DEVELOPMENT IN PRACTICE

# Sustaining Rapid Development in East Asia and the Pacific

# Sustaining Rapid Development in East Asia and the Pacific

THE WORLD BANK
WASHINGTON, D.C.

Manufactured in the United States of America
First printing March 1993

The Development in Practice series publishes reviews of the World Bank's activities in different regions and sectors. It lays particular emphasis on the progress that is being made and on the policies and practices that hold the most promise of success in the effort to reduce poverty in the developing world.

The findings, interpretations, and conclusions expressed in this study are entirely those of the authors and should not be attributed in any manner to the World Bank, to its affiliated organizations, or to members of its Board of Executive Directors or the countries they represent.

The denominations, classifications, boundaries, and colors used in the map do not imply on the part of the World Bank any judgment on the legal or other status of any territory or any endorsement or acceptance of any boundary.

*Library of Congress Cataloging-in-Publication Data*

Sustaining rapid development in East Asia and the Pacific.
p. cm. — (Development in practice)
Includes bibliographical references.
ISBN 0-8213-2386-5
1. East Asia—Economic conditions. 2. East Asia—Economic policy. 3. Pacific Area—Economic conditions. 4. Pacific Area—Economic policy. I. International Bank for Reconstruction and Development. II. Series: Development in practice (Washington, D.C.)
HC460.5.S88 1993
338.95—dc20 93-3075
CIP

This report, prepared by the Office of the Vice President, East Asia and Pacific Region, is based on the economic and operational work in the region and other parts of the World Bank. The principal authors were Ramgopal Agarwala and Vinod Thomas. Important contributions were made by Brandon Carter, Jeffrey Hammer, Osamu Kawaguchi, Deena Khatkhate, Kali Kondury, and Vikram Nehru. The authors also drew on the work of Frida Johansen, Anthony Rowley, and Subroto Roy. The report was produced under the general guidance of Gautam Kaji.

Many people in and outside the Bank provided valuable comments and contributions. Data from the International Economics Department were the basis for the regional development indicators. The support staff of the report included Carmencita Clay, Okie Moon Dorian, and Jae Shin Yang. Bruce Ross-Larson was the principal editor.

# Foreword

THE countries of East Asia and the Pacific have been at the leading edge of economic development in many respects over the past quarter century. Progress on some fronts has been so remarkable that policymakers around the world are searching for the lessons of East Asia's successes. But equally, the region—which is home to two-fifths of the population of the developing world—also faces tough economic problems and growing challenges.

Most of our work in the region is country-focused. Yet a regional survey such as this can bring out commonalities as well as differences that can inform country analysis. A regional assessment can also shed light on emerging problems that have a regional or global dimension—be it trade and investment or infrastructure and the environment. A regional overview can bring perspectives that would help in the design and implementation of country strategies. And, indeed, this report brings out a number of such insights.

First, despite the diversity among countries, East Asia has achieved remarkable performance in economic growth, poverty reduction, and social development, including a narrowing of the gender gap. And it has managed to do that not only during periods of substantial government interventions but even more spectacularly during the period of market reforms. Behind this performance lies a uniquely pragmatic and effective style of economic management that steers clear of theoretical abstracts and ideological extremes. This approach to economic management characterizes the socialist economies in transition such as China and Viet Nam as much as it does the market economies such as the Republic of Korea and Malaysia. The region now faces some difficult medium-term challenges, but I am confident that if policymakers in the region can continue their pragmatic management, East Asia will make history by being the first developing region to overcome the poverty problem.

Second, this regional development review brings into sharp focus the changing character of the region. Typically, one thinks of East Asia as a predominantly market-oriented and middle-income region. However, 80 percent of East Asia's population lives in socialist economies in transition, three times as many as live in the socialist economies in Eastern Europe and the former Soviet Union (FSU). Accordingly, the analytical challenges as well as resource requirements for the East Asia region during the 1990s will be enormous.

Third, even though East Asian economies have been undergoing reforms during the 1980s, the remaining reform agenda is still large and complex. In particular, the region needs to make a breakthrough during the 1990s in enterprise and financial sector reforms. Moreover, during the process of rapid growth, the region has accumulated serious problems of infrastructural bottlenecks, urban congestion, and pollution. And whereas East Asia is relatively successful in addressing some environmental concerns such as clean water, it has a long way to go in confronting the severe environmental problems such as air pollution, soil erosion, and deforestation.

Fourth, the report shows a sharp change in the external financing needs of the region. During the past twenty-five years the region has, on average, run current account deficits of less than 1 percent of its gross domestic product (GDP), although there were large variations among countries. But emerging deficits are much larger. These trends may continue in the region during the 1990s as it tackles its infrastructure problems and environmental issues. Equally striking is the fact that the external resource requirements for the socialist economies in the region that are moving toward market orientation are increasing, much as they have in Eastern Europe and the FSU.

Finally, the report emphasizes the interaction between domestic efforts and global developments. The external trade and resource requirements for growth highlight the crucial importance of greater openness in the regional and global environment for trade, investment, and capital flows. As pressures are mounting for regionalism and protectionism in the world, East Asia has a global leadership role to play in ensuring that the outward orientation of all parties is furthered. And within this region, the countries can gain substantially from concerted efforts at promoting intraregional trade and foreign direct investment.

This report is based on economic and sector work as well as operational work carried out in the region in recent years. In preparing the report, the authors have also drawn on views and analysis in the countries of the region. I expect that this report will be circulated and discussed widely within the region, and I look forward to a continuing process of interaction with our development partners in the region.

Gautam Kaji
Vice President
East Asia and Pacific Region

# Contents

## Figures



## Map 

## Text Tables



## Boxes



## Regional Development Indicators Tables

# Executive Summary

THE East Asia and Pacific region had a flying start to the 1990s with average output per capita expanding by 5.2 percent in 1990 and 5.6 percent in 1991, compared with a decline for the developing world on average. Over the past quarter century, per capita incomes in East Asia have nearly quadrupled, with a sharp reduction in poverty and notable progress in social development and in reducing the gender gap. Indeed, with absolute poverty now down to about 11 percent of the population, East Asia could almost eliminate poverty and close the social gap with the industrial countries within a generation or so—if it can meet the emerging challenges of the 1990s and sustain its rapid, broadly based growth and social development.

The region's solid economic performance has as its basis a strong outward orientation and an emphasis on human resource development, in addition to very effective institutional frameworks. In the past twenty-five years, current account deficits of the region as a whole have been surprisingly small—less than 1 percent of gross domestic product (GDP). And development was largely self financed, although many countries required and benefited from large external capital inflows, including foreign direct investment.

Compared with other regions, performance in East Asia was very good in the era of intervention (1965–80) and even better in the era of market reform (1980–90). East Asian governments are known to have intervened efficiently; less well known is the even greater success with market reforms in the 1980s. Both the state and the market have been important, with the state supporting markets, not supplanting them. This success has sparked interest among policymakers everywhere, who ask: how and why?

East Asia is not a story of unqualified success, however. It would be a great mistake for the region to become complacent or for the development community to neglect the region's problems. Not all East Asian countries have done well, and the spectrum of performance is wide—wider than in South Asia. Moreover, even the good performers have made costly errors in their policy and investment decisions. Vigilance, pragmatism, and flexibility—the main features of East Asia's solid performers—must continue for success to be sustained.

---

*East Asia could almost eliminate poverty and close the social gap with the industrial countries within a generation or so—if...*

---

## An Evolving Taxonomy of Countries

Despite the region's diversity, its problems for the 1990s can be analyzed by country groups and common challenges. Reflecting different stages of development and different development problems and prospects, the Bank's borrowers in East Asia fall into three groups.

- *The Asian tigers*: Republic of Korea (hereafter Korea), Malaysia, and Thailand. They have been growing rapidly over the past quarter century, and they now belong to the top third in the per capita income ranking of the developing world. For them the dominant question is how to sustain their dramatic growth. If they address issues of competitiveness, environment, infrastructure, and global trade, they have good prospects for sustaining their performance.

- *The socialist economies in transition*: They have roughly 80 percent of the population of East Asia, and they belong to the poorest third in the per capita income ranking of the developing world. Their total population is nearly three times that in Eastern Europe including the former Soviet Union (FSU). Even excluding China, socialist economies in East Asia have a significantly larger population than the countries of Eastern Europe (excluding the FSU), which have received so much world attention in recent years. No country has finished its socialist transformation. China is probably the most successful thus far, but it too has to deal with serious problems in reforming state-owned enterprises, containing regional income inequalities, and further alleviating poverty. Others—the Lao People's Democratic Republic, Mongolia, and Viet Nam—are undertaking bold but difficult measures to achieve stability and sustained growth.

Their efforts will succeed only if their strong domestic reform efforts can be combined with substantial concessional assistance (10–15 percent of their GDP) during the 1990s. Myanmar and the Democratic People's Republic of Korea will also need similar assistance when they decide to launch their reform programs—as will Cambodia. During the 1990s, these socialist economies in transition will dominate the Bank's analytical work and lending operations in the region.

■ *The island economies of the region, both large and small*: Indonesia, the Philippines, Papua New Guinea, and the Pacific islands. Because of their geography, they face special development challenges—in particular, interisland transport is expensive. By and large, they belong to the middle third in per capita income ranking of the developing countries. With the important exception of Indonesia, these economies have had poor growth during the 1980s, and strong efforts are needed to achieve decent growth. Per capita growth in the Philippines during the 1980s was poorer than that of Sub-Saharan Africa. Other island economies, including Papua New Guinea, have also experienced declining per capita incomes in the 1980s. In addition to sustained policy reforms, these countries will need external resources in the 1990s on a scale much larger than they received during the 1980s. Indonesia's growth performance was impressive, but it too faces some difficult issues in maintaining stability in its internal and external balances.

---

*During the 1990s, these socialist economies in transition will dominate the Bank's analytical work and lending operations in the region.*

---

## Four Challenges for the 1990s

During the 1990s, the region will have to address several cross-cutting challenges, four of which are highlighted in this report: removing bottlenecks in infrastructure, propelling the reform of state enterprises, completing the reform of the financial sector, and resolving environmental problems. Each is important for most of the countries of the region, but they differ somewhat in their intensity from country to country.

■ Most East Asian economies face infrastructure bottlenecks that can be overcome only with sizable investments. In some respects, this is a question of

*During the 1990s, the region will have to address several cross-cutting challenges, four of which are highlighted in this report: removing bottlenecks in infrastructure, propelling the reform of state enterprises, completing the reform of the financial sector, and resolving environmental problems.*

meeting the infrastructural demands of exceptionally rapid growth. In others, it is the result of past neglect. To meet this challenge, an enhanced role for the private sector and vigorously applied economic pricing principles must be combined with increased resource mobilization.

■ Public enterprise reform is—and will remain for the rest of this decade—an important priority for many countries of East Asia. This is true for socialist economies that are in transition from a centralized command system to a decentralized market system. And it is true for other countries with large public sectors and difficult public finance situations. The reform of state-owned enterprises ought to be approached pragmatically and considered part of a larger package of enterprise development efforts. Among other measures in such a package are fostering private sector development and competition among enterprises (public and private); privatizing state-owned enterprises and activities that were previously public monopolies; and strengthening the financial sector's ability to finance increased private sector capital requirements and to extend loans to state-owned enterprises on commercial terms, without government guarantees. In most countries of the region, sound strategies for enterprise reform need to address these three areas, with the emphasis depending on circumstances.

■ The important agenda for financial sector reforms is large and unfinished. Most East Asian countries launched some programs of financial liberalization in the 1980s. But in most cases, the passage has been rough, often with very high real interest rates and sometimes with disruptions in the corporate and financial sector. The reforms must be continued in the 1990s, and countries will have to coordinate them much more closely with macroeconomic stability and develop the capacity for prudent financial regulation.

■ Rapid growth generates resources for tackling environmental problems, and East Asia's growth has created just such opportunities. There has been good progress in addressing some environmental issues, such as clean water. But East Asia's environmental performance has generally been lagging. Among the developing regions, it has the highest rate of deforestation, the highest intensity of energy use per unit of GDP, and the highest emission rate of carbon dioxide per unit of GDP. It faces serious problems of sanitation in urban areas and of soil degradation in rural areas. Innovative actions now being initiated in the region need to be strengthened, and it is imperative that the government and the private sector seal a partnership to deal with the region's environmental challenges.

## Global Perspectives and Regional Priorities

In view of East Asia's outward orientation, the sluggish outlook on global economic growth and trade is a matter of serious concern for the region. Global GDP declined in 1991, and the decline was expected to continue in 1992 with only a modest recovery in 1993. Moreover, the underlying long-term output growth in the world economy is now slower, and sluggish growth rates in the industrial countries are strengthening protectionist tendencies and regionalism.

East Asia faces a choice: to form a regional bloc or to provide leadership in maintaining an open multilateral trade system. Given the diversity of countries in the region and the economic risks of looking inward, the East Asian countries do not consider a regional bloc to be appropriate. Integration is taking place in the region without any institutional structure through market-oriented foreign direct investment and trade flows—a process to be encouraged. Furthermore, East Asia can strengthen such integration through concerted trade liberalization and promotion of foreign direct investment in the region within the framework of the multilateral trading system. Concerted liberalization would involve regional consultations leading to reforms by East Asian countries in tandem, but would not mean exclusionary trade restrictions. Such regional efforts at trade liberalization on the part of East Asia will be realistic and effective, however, only if regional groups in other parts of the world remain consistent with the General Agreement on Tariffs and Trade (GATT) and do not become exclusionary.

*Resources, both domestic and external, must be mobilized on a scale the region has not needed in the past—to meet the new challenge of socialist transition.*

Despite East Asia's success in recent decades, the 1990s are not going to be an easy time for the region. Difficult policy reforms must be deepened and sustained. Resources, both domestic and external, must be mobilized on a scale the region has not needed in the past—to meet the new challenge of socialist transition as well as other old and new structural problems. But with the determination of its policymakers and the openness of its regional and global partners in development, there is every reason to believe that the 1990s will be another decade of solid performance.

CHAPTER ONE

# The Region's Economic Performance

WITH per capita incomes nearly quadrupling in the past twenty-five years, the East Asia and Pacific region has set a development record without precedent.[1] And that record holds valuable lessons for the region's future—and for other countries striving for rapid progress. It should be emphasized, however, that the region is far from homogeneous. It has countries at the top of the developing world (Korea, with more than $5,000[2] in per capita income) and at the bottom (Lao P.D.R., with less than $200). And it has China, with more than 1.1 billion[3] people, at one end and small island economies, with fewer than 100,000 people, at the other. Even within a single country, such as China or Indonesia, there are large regional variations.

The emerging issues of the region are evident for three broad country groups (chapter 2). First are the high fliers—Korea, Malaysia, and Thailand—at the upper end of the developing country income group (at or above the 60th percentile in per capita income among the developing countries). The other high fliers—Hong Kong, Singapore, and Taiwan (China)—are not considered here, as they now belong to the high-income group. All these economies have been growing fast—and they can be expected during the 1990s to move rapidly toward higher incomes. The main question is how to sustain their dramatic growth. A second distinct group comprises socialist economies in transition—Cambodia, China, Lao P.D.R., Mongolia, and Viet Nam and, perhaps, the Democratic People's Republic of Korea and Myanmar. Most are at the lower end of the per capita income league, and all are undertaking a transition without precedent.[4] The third consists of the island economies, large and small: Indonesia, Papua New Guinea, the Philippines, and smaller Pacific island economies. By

*With per capita incomes nearly quadrupling in the past twenty-five years, the East Asia and Pacific region has set a development record without precedent.*

and large, they belong to the middle range (from the 30th to 60th percentile) of per capita income rankings among the developing countries. With the important exception of Indonesia, their per capita income growth rate in the 1980s has been moderate or negative. They need to become more competitive in the 1990s and to generate growth in per capita incomes.

## A Flying Start to the 1990s

The region kicked off the 1990s with more of its spectacular performance (figure 1.1). Per capita growth in GDP for East Asia and the Pacific was about 5.2 percent in 1990 and 5.5 percent in 1991,[5] compared with a decline in average

FIGURE 1.1 EAST ASIA'S PERFORMANCE EDGE

***East Asia has been resilient to global recessions.***

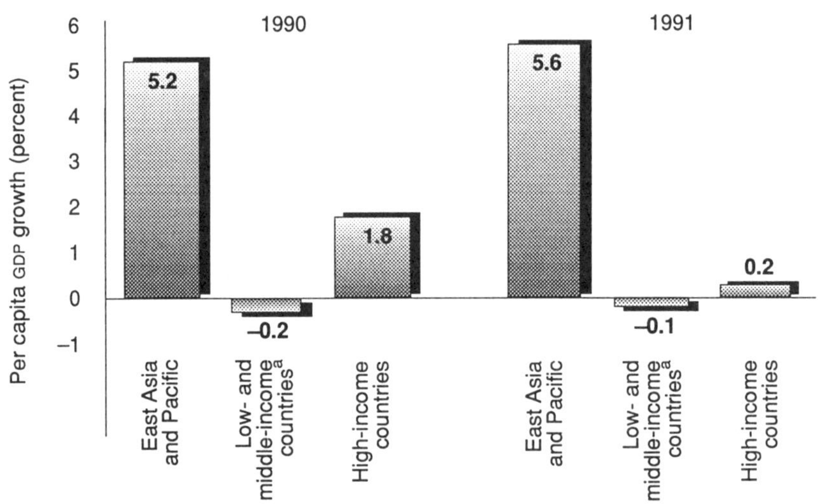


a. Includes former Soviet Union and Republic of South Africa; also includes East Asia and the Pacific.
*Source:* World Bank staff estimates.

output, the first in thirty years, for all developing countries. Preliminary indications are that 1992 will have seen a similar expansion in output for the region.

At the beginning of 1990, the future looked very different. Growth of world output and trade, crucial to East Asia's performance, was slowing. Protectionism was growing in industrial countries. And progress in the GATT negotiations was slow. There were domestic concerns, too. But excepting the Philippines, the region turned in a good performance. Malaysia led the way, with GDP growth of 8.8 percent in 1991. China, Indonesia, Korea, and Thailand were close behind, with growth ranging from 6.4 percent to 8.4 percent (table 1.1). Even in a year that saw little growth in world trade, these countries saw double-digit growth in export volume, thanks to their outward-oriented policies, with significant diversification in products and markets, and to increased intraregional trade. Similar double-digit growth in exports was also expected for 1992, although there are limits to how much intraregional trade can compensate for global trade.

## Dramatic Socioeconomic Gains

In the past twenty-five years, East Asia and the Pacific increased output at more than 7 percent a year and per capita output at more than 5 percent a year, with a near quadrupling of living standards. Korea doubled its per capita output in the eleven years from 1966 to 1977. China did the same in the ten years from 1977 to 1987. At roughly 9 percent a year, the region's exports in the past twenty-five years have risen twice as fast as those for the developing world as a group. As a result, exports quadrupled and accounted for about a third of GDP. Underlying

TABLE 1.1 GDP GROWTH, 1965–92
(annual percentage change, constant local currency)

***East Asia maintains growth momentum, with some exceptions.***

| *Country* | *1965–90* | *1990* | *1991* | *1992*[a] |
|---|---|---|---|---|
| China | 7.6 | 5.1 | 6.4 | 10.5 |
| Indonesia | 6.9 | 7.2 | 6.6 | 5.5 |
| Korea | 8.8 | 9.2 | 8.4 | 7.0 |
| Malaysia | 6.7 | 9.8 | 8.8 | 8.5 |
| Thailand | 7.1 | 10.3 | 8.0 | 7.5 |
| Philippines | 3.9 | 2.4 | –1.0 | 2.0 |

a. Preliminary estimate.
*Source:* World Bank staff estimates.

these trends was a deep structural transformation, with industry's share of GDP growing from a third to half.

The already large gap between the economic performance of East Asia and that of the rest of the developing world (save for South Asia, which also improved its performance) widened in the 1980s. Compared with the average for developing countries, East Asia did much better during 1965–80. Its relative performance improved further (and spectacularly) in the 1980s for three indicators—GDP, investment, and exports.

*The already large gap between the economic performance of East Asia and that of the rest of the developing world widened in the 1980s, save for South Asia, which also improved its performance.*

Underlying East Asia's growth were high levels of saving and investment. Its 1965 savings rate was about 22 percent of GDP. By 1991, it had risen to a spectacular 35 percent, roughly 60 percent more than the average for industrial countries. The savings rates are particularly high for China, Indonesia, Korea, Malaysia, and Thailand, and Korea's rates have reached the level of Japan's.

Rapidly rising domestic saving enabled East Asia to increase investment without resorting to large foreign saving. Over the past twenty-five years, investment rose at about 11 percent a year—roughly 50 percent faster than GDP growth. It is striking that for the region as a whole over this period, the net inflow of foreign saving was a modest 0.3 percent of GDP. There were, of course, variations in foreign capital inflows from year to year and from country to country. In many countries, the gross inflows of foreign capital (including direct foreign investment) were substantial, playing a crucial role in their development.

Compared with countries elsewhere, East Asia had self-reliant growth—and that self-reliance contributed to its relative freedom from the debt crisis and from the painful adjustment programs typical for many other countries in the 1980s. The relatively good record on debt servicing helped in turn to sustain voluntary capital inflows when needed. The near-match of saving and investment over time reflected the absence of large fiscal deficits or rapid monetary expansions. As a result, inflation was kept to single digits on average over the past twenty-five years, even when inflation in the rest of the developing world was in double digits.

To eliminate poverty is the overarching objective of development—and for many countries, a distant dream. Not so for East Asia, where the percentage of population below the absolute poverty line had fallen to about 10 percent by 1990. Over the past twenty-five years or so, absolute poverty has been brought down on average by more than one percentage point a year even as population expanded by some 2 percent a year. But the absolute number of poor is still large—about 180 million—and large numbers of people are estimated to be living just above the poverty line. Following present trends, the region could eliminate absolute poverty (as Korea and Malaysia have essentially done) within a generation or so, but only if rapid and broadly based growth can be sustained and inroads made into the more stubborn poverty areas (box 1.1).

Progress has also been rapid in the social indicators of development—faster than in the rest of the developing world and fast approaching the levels of the industrial countries (table 1.2). Much of the progress in health, nutrition, and education is undoubtedly attributable to the rapid growth of income. But most of the countries in the region have also pursued deliberate policies to improve the quality of life and the accumulation of human capital. Basic public goods—such as water supply and sanitation services, pest control, and public health information campaigns—have contributed to improvements in the health of the population, as has the provision of primary health care. Immunization rates have increased as a result and constitute a major reason for the improvement in the infant mortality rates. Most of the countries have vigorously pursued the goal of universal primary education, leading to enrollment rates that already match those of the high-income countries. And adult literacy rates will rise naturally with the next generation.

Over the years, the gender gap has been narrowed in many areas of social development in the region. Life expectancy at birth in the region as a whole is estimated to be higher for women (70 years) than for men (67 years), and the mortality rate for children under five years old lower for girls (37 per 1,000 live births) than for boys (48). As most East Asian countries achieved universal primary education, enrollment ratios for girls have approached those for boys. However, the completion rate to grade 4 remains lower for girls than for boys. Also, the adult illiteracy rate is estimated to be more than 30 percent for women, about twice as high as that for men. Clearly, much remains to be done in reducing the gender gap further and in improving the status of women.

---

*Over the past twenty-five years or so, absolute poverty in East Asia has been brought down on average by more than one percentage point a year.*

---

**BOX 1.1 POVERTY IN EAST ASIA**

High economic growth rates in East Asia in the 1980s contributed to equally impressive reductions in absolute poverty and improvements in social conditions. There were two distinguishing features of East Asian development that contributed to sharp reduction in poverty. First, economic growth was not only high—it was also broadly based. Second, public expenditures were effectively channeled to social development and to assisting the poor.

The absolute poor are those people at or below an income that allows them to buy only subsistence levels in food and nonfood necessities (the absolute poverty line). Official estimates are often based on widely different definitions of the poverty line. To achieve homogeneity in the definition of poverty and derive meaningful regional aggregates and trends, an equivalent poverty line was used across countries in a recent Bank study. The food budget included in that line allows 2,150 calories per day per person, with 90 percent of the calories from grains that are the lowest-cost source of calories in East Asia (as in the official poverty lines in China and Indonesia) or other food choices costing the same. By this definition, there has been a dramatic decrease in absolute poverty in East Asia's developing countries—from a third of the population in 1970 to a fifth in 1980 and a tenth in 1990.

The two countries with the most people, China and Indonesia, made the most progress. Indonesia started the 1970s with more than half its people, some 70 million, in poverty, but by 1990 this had fallen to 15 percent (27 million). Korea and Malaysia—having made much progress by 1970—reached out to the increasingly marginal poor, many of whom are normally bypassed by overall economic growth, and ended 1990 with fewer than 5 percent of their people in poverty.

Through the 1970s and 1980s, Thailand had some 9 million absolute poor, and the Philippines 13 million. But both countries reduced the incidence of absolute poverty by about a third, to 16 percent in Thailand and 20 percent in the Philippines. Thailand's incidence is estimated to be similar to that of Indonesia, even though its average gross national product (GNP) per capita is some 2.5 times higher.

**EAST ASIA'S ESTIMATED REDUCTION IN ABSOLUTE POVERTY, 1970–90**

| *Year* | *Incidence (percent)* | *Number (milllions)* |
|---|---|---|
| 1970 | 35 | 400 |
| 1980 | 23 | 300 |
| 1990 | 10 | 180 |

*Note*: These estimates are based on comparable poverty lines for Cambodia, China, Indonesia, Korea, Lao P.D.R., Malaysia, the Philippines, Thailand, and Viet Nam.

*Source*: Johansen 1992.

TABLE 1.2 PROGRESS IN MEETING BASIC NEEDS

***East Asia on average can close the social gap with the industrial countries within a generation.***

| | East Asia and Pacific region | | High-income countries |
|---|---|---|---|
| *Indicator* | *1965* | *1990* | *1990* |
| Daily calorie supply (per capita) | 1,939 | 2,617[a] | 3,416[a] |
| Enrollment rate in primary school (percent) | 88 | 100+[a] | 100+[a] |
| Adult illiteracy rate (percent) | — | 24 | 4 |
| Infant mortality rate (per thousand) | 95 | 34 | 8 |
| Total fertility rate (per woman) | 6.2 | 2.7 | 1.7 |
| Life expectancy at birth (years) | 51 | 68 | 77 |

— Not available.
a. Data are for 1989.
*Note:* Recent estimates are lacking for many countries, so regional averages should be treated only as illustrative.
*Source:* World Bank 1992d and 1992e.

The 1980s have been a decade of impressive gains in family planning programs in East Asia. Today, knowledge and use of contraception are widespread in most East Asian countries, family planning services are often accessible, and many of the easiest-to-reach people are already served. The projected population growth between 1990 and 2030 is thus estimated at 50 percent, as against the doubling over the preceding forty years. In absolute terms, however, the number is large: an increase of about 1 billion people. Strong family planning programs must thus be continued, particularly in countries at earlier stages of the fertility decline, such as Malaysia, Papua New Guinea, Thailand, and Viet Nam. Even more important now are factors that provide incentives to have smaller families: increased access for women to education and employment, and higher family incomes.

The agenda in providing basic services to the poor is far from finished. Safe water and sanitation services need to be extended further. The changing requirements of the education system need to be addressed as countries achieve universal primary education and grapple with ways of attaining a skilled work force in a competitive world economy. Without underplaying the problems ahead, one can say that the progress in human resource development suggests that governments will meet the challenges.

One problem that demands urgent attention is the growing threat of AIDS. While not yet reaching the disastrous proportions of the epidemic in Africa, the disease has been spreading rapidly in Asia, and the potential is great for much worse to come. The World Health Organization predicts that by 2000, 40 million people will be infected with HIV worldwide, with half of these in Asia and over 6 million in Thailand alone. Governments should begin immediately to think of ways to head off the disease. The problem is already recognized as a crisis in Thailand, and the other countries in the region could face similar futures if it is not contained.

## The Search for Lessons from East Asia

There is a widespread interest in knowing the secrets of East Asia's success. What policies contributed to East Asia's remarkable progress? Why were these policies adopted? Did policies similar to those adopted elsewhere produce better results—and if so, why?

---

*Political commitment, consensus building, the drive to participate in the global economy, the great effectiveness of institutional structures, and discipline, flexibility, and pragmatism in the approach to development— all of these were crucial to East Asia's overall performance.*

---

The political commitment for putting priority on economic development, building consensus for designing economic policies, the drive to participate in the global economy, the great effectiveness of institutional structures, and discipline, flexibility, and pragmatism in the approach to development—all of these were crucial to East Asia's overall performance. And perception is growing today that East Asia not only adopted better policies—it also managed to get more mileage out of its policy framework.

*World Development Report 1991* (World Bank 1991) elaborated four general features of East Asian policies and interventions that are important for future development in the region and elsewhere. First, these economies were noted for their outward orientation. Either by design or necessity, economies such as Korea, Malaysia, and Thailand made a commitment to be players in the global economy. Striving to be a force in the global market encouraged discipline and efficiency—and provided valuable checks and balances to all interventions.

Second, East Asia made sizable and efficient investments in people. This was key not only to rapid economic growth, but also to extraordinary social progress. East Asia's quantity and quality of spending on education and health compare favorably with other regions—and, combined with the openness to the world, provided especially high payoffs.

Third, the macroeconomic discipline of the public sector set an example for the entire economy. Public sector discipline in spending ensured that rents from government interventions were minimized. Some economies such as Thailand set legal limits on government deficits. Others—such as China, Korea, and Malaysia—were quick to respond to growing deficits with stabilization policies.

And fourth, institutional development was crucial to the success. The state supported the market, rather than supplanting it. A large sample of countries shows that those with fewer macroeconomic and price distortions (such as East Asian countries) do better. But government interventions in the economy in this East Asian subgroup were by no means small. Government spending as a fraction of GDP, for example, was as high as the international averages. But the effectiveness of the spending, and of government intervention in general, was greater.

The surge in interest in the region's accomplishment—and the role of public policy in this accomplishment—has prompted a major World Bank study, with Japanese collaboration, of the East Asian experience, scheduled for completion in 1993. The focus of the study is the link between public policy and economic growth in high-performing East Asian economies and the replicability of the East Asian approach for other developing countries. The study has four main objectives:

- To provide an overview of the process of growth in the high-performing East Asian economies by analyzing patterns of output growth, structural change, and productivity growth in each economy

- To describe the strategic approaches of governments to promote rapid growth, the rationale for undertaking them, and the sequencing, objectives, and outcomes of individual policy measures

- To evaluate how much the rate and pattern of growth are attributable to public policy

- To assess whether successful interventions in the East Asian economies are replicable in other developing countries.

The research covers Indonesia, Japan, Korea, Malaysia, Singapore, and Thailand. One country case study is undertaken for each, except Japan, for which a collection of several essays on aspects of public policy in the rapid growth period is planned. In addition, comparative studies are undertaken independent of the country studies—to address trade and industrial policies, financial markets and policies, human capital and labor markets, and institutional structures and innovations.

CHAPTER TWO

# An Evolving Taxonomy of Countries

THE stellar performance of the East Asia region is cause for confidence, but not for complacency. The full story of East Asia is not one of undifferentiated success. Indeed, the performance variation is greater in East Asia than in South Asia. In the 1980s, GDP growth in South Asia was between 4.0 percent a year (Sri Lanka) and 6.3 percent (Pakistan). In East Asia, it was less than 1 percent a year in Myanmar and the Philippines, but 7 percent or more for the high fliers, such as China, Korea, and Thailand (figure 2.1).

Even among the high-performance economies in the 1980s—China, Indonesia, Korea, Malaysia, and Thailand—the variation was wide. A part of the strong performance of East Asia in the 1980s was due to China. If China is excluded, East Asia had slowdowns in the 1980s in growth of GDP, industry, investment, and exports—even though *relative* to other regions, there was an improvement (see appendix table 28).

On the basis of the stage of development, past trends, and current outlook for the future, the region can be divided into three groups of countries:[6]

- Asian tigers
- Socialist economies in transition
- Island economies, large and small.

## Asian Tigers

With the graduation of Hong Kong, Singapore, and Taiwan (China) to high-income rank, the Asian tigers now consist of three dynamic countries of the region: Korea, Malaysia, and Thailand. Over the past twenty-five years, they

*The full story of East Asia is not one of undifferentiated success. Indeed, the performance variation is greater in East Asia than in South Asia.*

have made spectacular progress, though few credited them with such rosy prospects in the 1950s (box 2.1). They account for only 7 percent of the region's population, but because their incomes are so high, they greatly influence the regional averages of income.

Combining rapid and broadly based growth with active social development programs, Korea and Malaysia virtually eliminated poverty by 1990 (see box 1.1). In Thailand there has been substantial poverty reduction in the past three decades, but progress has been slow in the 1980s despite rapid economic growth. This is in part due to growing disparities in income in Thailand, discrimination against agriculture, and the lagging expenditures in social sectors in recent years despite large fiscal surpluses.

These economies share commonalities of approach and are increasingly the subject of attention for other developing countries. But their policies have also

FIGURE 2.1 AVERAGE ANNUAL GROWTH OF GDP, 1980–90

***East Asia had a wide spectrum of growth in the 1980s—wider than in South Asia.***

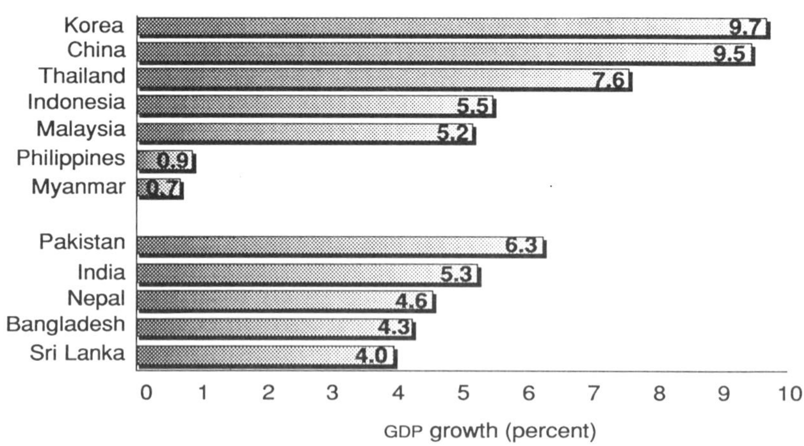


*Source*: World Bank 1992e; World Bank staff estimates.

varied over time and among themselves. These variations relate to resource endowments, which affect macroeconomic balances and the role of government and of external capital inflows. The political systems also varied enormously. Korea was under military rule for most of the period. Malaysia was a politically stable democracy. Thailand was a constitutional monarchy with a democratically elected government, repeatedly overthrown by military coups.

On the role of government, Korea was the most interventionist: the financial sector was nationalized, import controls and import substitution were widely practiced, the public sector was a big part of the economy, and the government intervened heavily in private-sector investment and trade. In Malaysia and Thailand, the private sector was dominant in producing goods, whereas the government concentrated on social and physical infrastructure. Of the three, the Malaysian government intervened most to alter the distribution of income and wealth.

Korea had high double-digit inflation during 1965–80, whereas Thailand and Malaysia kept inflation in low single figures. Although all three economies had an outward-oriented policy, growth of exports in relation to GDP during this period varied largely—in Korea, exports grew 2.7 times faster than GDP, whereas in Malaysia they grew slower than GDP. All three had high investment growth, but the sources of financing were different. In 1965–80, Korea's savings rate was the lowest (19 percent of GDP), and it relied heavily on external capital inflows (7 percent of GDP) but with very little foreign private investment. Malaysia and Indonesia had significant surpluses on their external resource balance, while Thailand ran a modest deficit of about 3 percent of GDP.

Despite their impressive performance over the long term, all three Asian tigers need to continue their reform efforts and be vigilant about changing circumstances. One area of immediate concern is rising current account deficits. Until recently, these three countries were running a surplus in their current account ($14.3 billion in 1988); within three years, there was a $35 billion shift in their current account balance. By 1991, they were running a deficit of $21.1 billion (table 2.1). About a fifth of these inflows was funded by (non-debt-creating) foreign direct investment, but there has also been a sharp increase in short- and long-term debt flows. The debt service ratios for all three countries are low (about 10 percent), and there is no immediate cause for alarm. But these

*Despite their impressive performance over the long term, all three Asian tigers need to continue their reform efforts and be vigilant about changing circumstances.*

**BOX 2.1 EAST ASIA'S PROSPECTS AS SEEN IN THE 1950S**

In the 1950s, the *Philippines* was the best performer among East Asian economies and was widely regarded as the most promising for the long-run. The Bank's economic report published in November 1957 concluded, ". . . The Philippines has achieved a rapid rate of economic growth in the post-war period, (since 1949). Production has continued to grow at an annual rate of 7 percent, despite the disrupting effects of the HUK movement, which hampered economic activity until 1952. . . . By comparison with most underdeveloped countries, the basic economic position of the Philippines is favorable. It has a generous endowment of arable land, forest resources, minerals and normal potential. Through a comparatively high level of expenditure on education, transport, communications and industrial plant over the past 50 years, the Philippines has achieved a position in the Far East second only to Japan, both in respect to its level of literacy, and to per capita production capacity. . . . The prospects of the Philippine economy for sustained long-term growth are good. [Apart from] generous endowment of material resources and high level of literacy, other favorable factors are the growth of the labor force, the availability of managerial and technical skills, the high level of savings and investment, rather good prospects for most of the Philippine exports, and considerable possibilities for import substitution."

Next most promising was *Myanmar* (then *Burma*), an apparent success story in the making. In 1953, the Bank's economic report concluded, "Prospects appear favorable for steady economic improvement. It seems reasonable to expect an accelerated rate of progress towards restructuring, diversifying and expanding the economy." By 1958, Burma's record was impressive and the Bank's report became even more bullish. "In her first 10 years of independence, Burma has made remarkable economic progress. Aggregate output has grown at a high rate—5 percent per year in the last five years—and a large share of resources has been set aside for capital formation. . . . Given the large amounts of readily available material resources and the absence of population pressure, given the high level of resources available for investment, Burma's long-run potential compares favorably with those of other countries in South East Asia."

trends show that there is no room for complacency, and even the best of performers must remain vigilant.

The three countries also face challenges in the areas of infrastructure, enterprise reforms, financial sector liberalization, environmental protection, and the changing global trade environment—challenges common to most East Asian countries. All three tigers can be expected to continue their rapid growth during the 1990s and to reduce their reliance on external assistance during the latter part of this decade. Korea has submitted a graduation plan to the Bank to phase out lending by fiscal 1995, and it is expected to become a contributor to devel-

At the other end of the spectrum was *Indonesia*. Its GDP growth in 1950–64 was 1.5 to 2.0 percent a year. The outlook was one of declining per capita income. The Bank's economic report in 1968 concluded, "Rather than attempt to say specifically where we think the economy is heading at the end of 10 years, it seems more profitable to indicate what may be required to produce a rate of growth at least above that of the population during the next few years."

*Korea* was another country with poor prospects. In the 1950s, Korea's economy grew by 4 to 5 percent a year, growth largely financed by foreign aid. Domestic savings were barely 3 percent of GNP, and exports were below $30 million a year. Prospects for development were anything but bright. The first plan prepared for 1962–66 projected growth of 7.1 percent a year and a tripling of export earnings by the end of the plan. The Bank mission stated: "There can be no doubt that this development program by far exceeds the potential of the Korean economy. In the first place, the projections of domestic savings are extremely ambitious. . . . It is inconceivable that exports will rise as much as projected."

In between were *Thailand* and *Malaysia*. In the 1950s, the Thai economy appeared to be sound but with little prospect of improvement in per capita incomes or industrial transformation. The Bank's economic reports in 1955 and 1956 concluded, "Basically Thailand's economy is sound. Population pressure is not great; and the undeveloped resources of the country are considerable. There are good reasons for supposing that sound economic policies within the long-run not only maintain the standard of living of the people but even raise it, despite the growth of population. . . . No basic changes in the structure of Thailand's economy have occurred for many years or appear to be in prospect. The government's program to diversify the economy somewhat is not likely to alter substantially the traditional pattern of foreign trade or distribution of resources and incomes within Thailand at least within the next few decades." The Bank's economic report on Malaysia published in 1958 concluded, "it should be possible for the Federation to maintain a pace of economic expansion at least equal to the prospective growth in population. There are, however, some uncertainties in this outlook."

opment finance in the latter half of the decade. Nor do Malaysia and Thailand seek high levels of financial assistance from the Bank. Instead, they seek selective lending and advice.

## Socialist Economies in Transition

The dominant concern of the region during the 1990s will be the socialist economies in transition—Cambodia, China, Lao P.D.R., Mongolia, Viet Nam, and, perhaps in the future, the Democratic People's Republic of Korea and

TABLE 2.1 CURRENT ACCOUNT BALANCE, 1988–91

***Even the best performers must remain vigilant about external deficits.***

| *Country* | *1988* | *1989* | *1990* | *1991* |
|---|---|---|---|---|
| *In billions of dollars* | | | | |
| Korea | 14.2 | 5.1 | –2.2 | –8.8 |
| Malaysia | 1.8 | –0.2 | –1.7 | –4.3 |
| Thailand | –1.7 | –3.6 | –8.4 | –8.0 |
| Total | 14.3 | 1.3 | –12.3 | –21.1 |
| *As percentage of GDP* | | | | |
| Korea | 8.3 | 2.4 | –0.9 | –3.0 |
| Malaysia | 5.2 | –0.6 | –3.9 | –9.3 |
| Thailand | –2.8 | –5.2 | –10.3 | –8.5 |

*Source:* World Bank staff estimates.

Myanmar. Together, they account for more than 80 percent of the region's people—and three times the population affected by the socialist transition in Eastern Europe (including the former Soviet Union). Even if China is excluded, the other socialist economies would represent about 170 million people, 20 percent more than in East European economies (excluding the FSU).

This group of countries is making a historic transition, with no past experience to build on. As in Eastern Europe and the FSU, the transition in East Asia is far from easy. While the East Asian socialist economies face similar transition problems as in Eastern Europe and the FSU, the substantial differences in the structure of these economies are noteworthy. First, the East Asian socialist economies are at a much earlier stage of development. Second, while the economies of Eastern Europe and the FSU are predominantly industrial, the East Asian socialist economies have a large agricultural sector—and small and medium-size industries play a key role in their industrial sector. These differences in initial conditions affect the pace and content of the reform processes in these countries. China has obtained solid results from reforms; others have a mixed record.

*China*'s program, started in 1979, has had four distinctive features:

- *Gradualism and experimentation.* Because of its large size, provincial structure, and primary concern for stability, China has opted for spreading changes over several years, usually after experimentation and adaptation.

*Together, the socialist economies in transition account for more than 80 percent of the region's people—and three times the population affected by the socialist transition in Eastern Europe (including the former Soviet Union).*

- *Partial reforms within sectors.* A two-tier price system allows marginal decisions based on market prices, and market skills can be learned without economic dislocation.

- *Decentralization of decisionmaking.* The decentralization of decisionmaking to enterprises, individuals, and local governments has enhanced microeconomic incentives and created a strong interest group that favors continuing to deepen the reform.

- *Self-reinforcing reforms.* Reforms in one area created pressures for matching reforms in other areas, and policymakers have generally seen their interests served best by meeting such pressures with new reforms (albeit sometimes with a considerable lag) rather than by invoking administrative protectionism.

China's approach to reform has been relatively effective:

- *Output and welfare.* GNP has grown about 50 percent faster during the reform period, especially in light industry and services. This has resulted in enormous improvements in consumption (it more than doubled over the decade) and in lifting an estimated 160 million people out of poverty since 1979.

- *Productivity.* Growth has come through productivity gains, which were close to zero in 1949–79 but accounted for 3 to 4 percent of annual growth during the reforms. These gains could have been even greater with further reforms, for example, in state enterprises.

- *The role of the state.* The state used to account for most savings and investment, but now, individuals and enterprises generate most savings; and investment is financed largely by retained profits and bank loans. State-owned enterprises used to account for almost all output in the prereform period. Today, nonstate industry employs almost 100 million people and produces 45 percent of industrial output.

- *Trade.* The share of trade in GNP has risen from just less than 10 percent in 1978 to more than 30 percent in 1990, and there are now more than 20,000 Sino-foreign joint ventures.

The crucial challenge that China now faces is the reform of state enterprises—in concert with reform in other areas of the economy. This is a tough issue for which proven solutions are not readily available in the context of a socialist economy.

Other problems of transition in socialist economies are inflation and unemployment, particularly urban unemployment. The socialist economies have typically minimized these problems at the cost of efficiency. During 1965–80 China had almost no inflation. With the freeing of markets, however, inflation was about 5 percent a year on average during the 1980s, reaching as high as 21 percent in 1988. Similar tradeoffs may be unavoidable in unemployment. Already, millions are coming to urban areas in search of work but are remaining in the pool of the unemployed. There is a large degree of repressed migration in China. As restrictions on labor mobility are eased, migration to cities will accelerate. With rapid income growth in coastal China, the poor and the near poor from inland will be attracted there by the promise of high incomes, even if the probability of getting work is low. So, in easing its labor market restrictions, China might also have to address a transitional phase of growing urban unemployment.

In *Mongolia* the government's reform program was launched in the face of several external shocks—a sharp decline in Soviet aid, collapse of trade among members of the socialist trading bloc, weak markets for Mongolia's hard-currency exports (cashmere, wool, and leather)—and a poor harvest. In 1991 external trade fell drastically, and shortages of key imported inputs, along with frequent electricity outages, led to a sharp decline in GDP and an alarming increase in urban unemployment. A tight monetary policy in 1991 was hurt by an inability to reduce the budget deficit, and, in stark contrast to decades-long price stability prior to 1990, inflation soared to between 120 and 150 percent.

*Lao P.D.R.* and *Viet Nam* have freed virtually all prices, raised interest rates, and devalued the exchange rate. After satisfactory growth in 1988 and 1989, Viet Nam faced difficulties in 1990 and 1991 as Soviet aid, which once totaled $1 billion a year, was cut off. The industrial sector stagnated, and inflation accelerated to between 60 and 70 percent. Still, GDP—buoyed by expanding agricultural output, growth in services, and a vigorously emerging private sector—grew by about 3 percent in 1991. In 1992 GDP growth accelerated and the inflation rate came down. Viet Nam's success in making reforms and achieving income growth despite external shocks and without any significant external assistance is impressive. But its domestic saving has been low, and this, combined with negligible foreign development assistance, has meant that the investment rate has been only 12 percent of GDP in recent years—an inadequate foundation for sustained growth. Lao P.D.R., on the other hand, has received substantial external assistance and maintained GDP growth of about 5 percent in 1991, with inflation falling to 10 percent (from 68 percent in 1989).

*Cambodia* faces an uphill struggle. Peace has returned, but the cost of twenty years of war has been high: assets have been demolished, communities dispersed, human resources destroyed, institutions debilitated, and incentives distorted. The economy needs to be stabilized, institutions built, and basic public services restored. Policy reforms need to be combined with substantial external assistance if the economy is to be revived. The authorities have initiated reforms, but these have been partial and ad hoc—and the results mixed. Food production has increased and informal industry and supporting services have been growing rapidly over the past three years. The resource crunch has been severe, however, leading to inflation of more than 100 percent a year in 1989–92. Foreign assistance from the now defunct Council for Mutual Economic Assistance (CMEA) ceased in 1990, and Western and international donors have not yet been able to fill the gap. The budget is in a crisis, with more than 45 percent of total expenditures unfunded.

The trend toward liberalization and privatization in the socialist countries is certainly a welcome development. During the transition period, however, the burdens of reform weigh heavily on the newly unemployed and other vulnerable groups. An increase in the inequality of income is a real possibility in many reforming countries. Both for promoting the welfare of the population and for the political sustainability of reform, maintaining essential social services and developing a reliable social safety net are required.

Privatization efforts should follow good economic analysis and must recognize priorities. Those sectors in which private markets work well, in which market failures are few, and which should never have been in public hands can safely be privatized. But many of the markets related to human resource development, particularly in health, are problem-ridden, and governments need to think through the implications of rapid privatization of such services.

---

*To tackle the social and economic problems of transition, the socialist economies in East Asia will require external resources in the 1990s on a scale far beyond what they have needed in the past.*

---

To tackle the social and economic problems of transition, the socialist economies in East Asia will require external resources in the 1990s on a scale far beyond what they have needed in the past. During the past twenty-five years, China achieved remarkable growth without any significant net external capital inflows. With the increased opening of the economy, imports are rising faster than exports. The repressed demand for consumer goods suggests that, with liberalization, the domestic savings rate might go down rather than up during the 1990s. Bank staff estimates indicate that China may need substantial external financial inflows (including foreign direct investment) during the 1990s, a significant departure from the past.

For Cambodia, Lao P.D.R., and Viet Nam, the external resource requirements in the 1990s are likely to be very large. While data on savings and investment in these economies are weak, they suggest that domestic savings are extremely low—ranging from 0 to 10 percent of GDP. Sustained growth in these economies will require investment rates of 20 to 25 percent of GDP during the 1990s. Thus, even allowing for some improvements in domestic resource mobilization, external financing of 10 to 15 percent of GDP can be regarded as essential for these economies during the 1990s.

Myanmar and the Democratic People's Republic of Korea have not yet launched their reform programs. If they do so during the 1990s, their external resource requirements could also be substantial.

## Island Economies, Large and Small

The third group consists of the island economies, both large and small. They account for 16 percent of the region's population. Their geography imposes certain special constraints on development. Infrastructure costs are particularly high, and communications difficult.

Indonesia, the dominant member of this group, has had relatively impressive performance, much better than seemed possible in the 1950s and early 1960s (see box 2.1). Over the twenty-five years since 1965, its per capita income has grown by 4.5 percent a year. And by 1990 it had succeeded in reducing the incidence of poverty to 15 percent, a remarkable achievement for its level of per capita income.

Among the factors that contributed to this remarkable achievement are the following:

- *Focus on agriculture.* In the early phase, the primary focus of the government's strategy was improving the productivity of the rural economy and, in particular, attaining self-sufficiency in rice. Agriculture, including irrigation, constituted more than one-third of the development budget during the first plan period, 1969–74.

*By 1990 Indonesia had succeeded in reducing the incidence of poverty to 15 percent, a remarkable achievement for its level of per capita income.*

■ *Public spending on social and physical infrastructure.* Since 1974, when public resources increased significantly, the government has expanded its productivity-enhancing outlays in rural areas: for agriculture, primary schools, health facilities, and roads. There has been little reliance on direct transfer programs, consumer subsidies, or public employment.

■ *Vigorous adjustments to external shocks.* When oil prices dropped in the 1980s, the government moved quickly to introduce adjustment measures. In agriculture, exchange rate depreciations cushioned the effects of lower export prices. In the manufacturing and service sectors, the combination of trade and industrial deregulation and real exchange rate adjustments led to a surge in non-oil exports and a rapid recovery in manufacturing growth and investment, as well as an increase in real wages and employment levels. In reducing public expenditure, public consumption was preserved to the extent necessary to make productive use of the infrastructure created. And expenditures in poverty-related sectors—agriculture, human resource development, and transfers to lower-level governments—were protected relative to public expenditures of less benefit to the poor (notably in industry and mining). As a result of these and other measures, the country's dependence on oil for budget revenues and exports has been sharply reduced.

Maintaining macroeconomic stability is a key issue in Indonesia as policymakers chart a narrow course between growth rapid enough to meet the aspirations of the people and growth that is too rapid for macroeconomic stability. Despite its large foreign-exchange earnings from oil and more recently from nontraditional exports, Indonesia has borrowed heavily from external sources. At the end of 1991 its external debt stood at $75 billion (66 percent of GDP), and its debt service ratio was 33 percent, comparable to countries with debt problems. In 1991 inflation was moderate (the consumer price index rose by 9.2 percent). The current account deficit—which reached $4.5 billion (about 4 percent of GDP)—was financed by commercial borrowings at increasingly stiff terms (that is, shorter maturities and higher spreads). In addition, some public and quasi-public bodies were planning in early 1991 to raise external capital for some large projects. Faced with possible strains on debt-servicing capacity, the government in September 1991 formed the Commercial Offshore Loan Team (COLT) for the coordination of all public and public-related borrowings. Subsequently, the team deferred four big projects and laid down ceilings for public, quasi-public, and commercial bank borrowings, as well as guidelines for prudent private-sector borrowings and improved reporting requirements. The Bank of Indonesia also limited domestic banks' non-trade-related short-term borrowings from abroad to a percentage of their capital base.

*The Philippines'* recent performance has not been impressive. In the 1950s, it was thought to have the best potential in the region, second only to Japan (see box 2.1). It achieved impressive growth rates in the 1950s and 1960s but then suffered setbacks in the 1980s, with declines in per capita income sharper even than those in Sub-Saharan Africa and Latin America.

The Philippines has been largely a private-sector-oriented economy. Its price distortions are relatively low; its effective protection is among the lowest in the region; it has a flexible exchange rate regime; and it has liberalized trade and the financial sector and privatized state-owned enterprises more than most of its well-performing neighbors. (See figure 2.2 for measures of effective protection rates in the Philippines compared with other major East Asian countries; and figure 2.3 for measures of the share of state enterprise investment.) It also has an excellent supply of labor—both skilled and unskilled. Now the need is to restore credibility and confidence in the country's ability to stay the course and get positive results. Among the key issues are:

FIGURE 2.2 EFFECTIVE PROTECTION RATES IN MANUFACTURING

***Some countries maintained their export competitiveness despite import protection.***

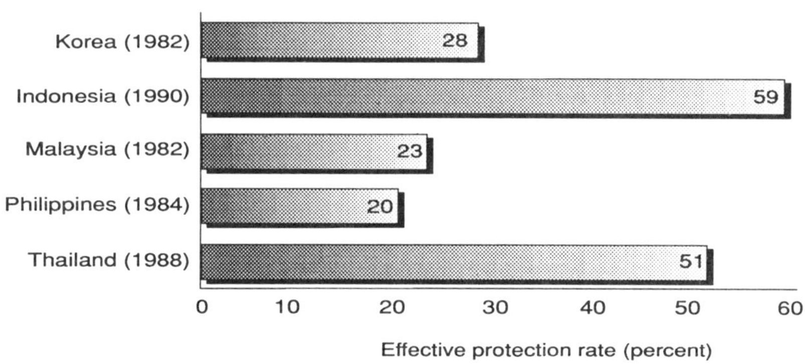


*Note:* Because of the differences in coverage and definitions, cross-country comparisons have their limitations.
*Source:* Bhattacharya and Linn 1988; World Bank data.

FIGURE 2.3 INVESTMENT IN STATE ENTERPRISES AS A PERCENTAGE OF TOTAL INVESTMENT

***The public sector's role varied enormously among countries and during periods with rapid growth.***

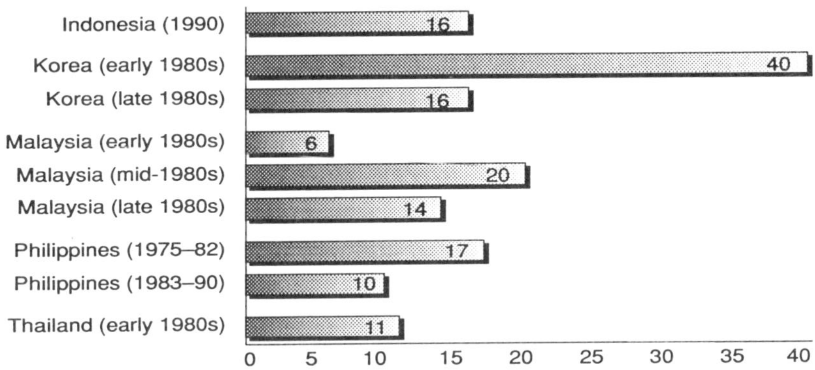


*Source:* World Bank data.

■ *Reviving investor confidence.* Foreign direct investment with an export orientation has been an important element in maintaining growth in Southeast Asian countries in the 1980s. During the second half of the 1980s Thailand and Malaysia received foreign direct investment of more than $1 billion a year, whereas the Philippines received less than $500 million.

■ *Rehabilitating infrastructure.* Critical to reviving private investment is improvement in infrastructure, particularly electricity and transport. Major changes are needed in pricing policies and investment programs.

■ *Ensuring macroeconomic stability.* Vigorous action is called for to increase tax revenue, which at 15 percent of GNP is lower than in other East Asian countries; lowering the high real interest rate of about 10 percent; and reducing the continuing high debt, with a public debt-to-GDP ratio of 0.9.

*Now the need in the Philippines is to restore credibility and confidence in the country's ability to stay the course and get positive results.*

*During the 1990s the shared development challenge for the smaller Pacific islands lies in channeling resources to growth in the few areas with a clear comparative advantage.*

- *Strengthening institutions.* Economic efficiency suffers from serious institutional weaknesses that cause implementation problems and from a lack of coordinated vision between government and business and between branches of government.

- *Reducing poverty.* The official estimate of absolute poverty in the Philippines—more than 50 percent—is overstated because of the use of a rather high poverty line. Nevertheless, even a more realistic poverty line suggests a higher incidence of poverty than in many other countries of similar or even lower per capita income.

*Papua New Guinea* and *small Pacific island economies,* accounting for about 0.3 percent of the region's population, present some special issues. Many belong to the middle-income group, but during the 1980s their per capita incomes have been declining, despite a high level of assistance and mineral wealth. For most of the last decade, private nonmineral investment in these countries was low, gains in productivity were limited, and international competitiveness was declining.

These economies must address difficult structural problems if they are to generate and sustain growth during the 1990s and beyond. During the run-up to independence, Papua New Guinea became saddled with a high-cost wage structure, as legislated minimum wages outpaced productivity and the groundwork was laid for a costly civil service that continues to dominate formal sector employment. To restore competitiveness, it will be essential to adopt a productivity-based wage-determination system to reduce real wages and narrow the urban-rural wage difference, a challenging task in view of sizable income and fiscal surpluses expected to arise from a boom in oil and mineral revenue starting in 1994.

For the smaller Pacific island economies the development issues have been analyzed by the Bank in two regional economic reports. In general, these economies have fallen short in stimulating private investment in productive sectors. During the 1990s their shared development challenge lies in channeling resources to growth in the few areas with a clear comparative advantage. Public policy can help the private sector identify areas of comparative advantage and profitable niches in domestic and world markets. The external environment in the 1990s is expected to remain difficult, with further erosion in relative prices of primary commodities. In view of structural problems and the external environment facing these economies, more effective donor support will be essential for steady growth in productive investment in these economies.

CHAPTER THREE

# Four Challenges for the 1990s

IF East Asia sustains its current pace of development, it will be the first developing region to eliminate absolute poverty. Such an outcome is far from automatic, however. The East Asian economies need to pursue their reform programs vigorously, applying their pragmatic and flexible approaches to old and new problems. The international community, in turn, needs to continue its partnership in providing financial and nonfinancial assistance to the region. Several old concerns—such as infrastructural development, enterprise reforms, and financial sector reform—will have to be addressed with new urgency. And new concerns—the rising environmental threat and the changing international trade arrangements—will test East Asia's innovative capacities.

These cross-cutting themes are the subject of this chapter. Human resource development, although a key issue in all countries, is not considered here as a special problem in view of the region's good performance. Urbanization, another major issue, is treated as part of infrastructural and environmental problems.

## Addressing Infrastructural Bottlenecks

The faster-growing economies of East Asia have been running into constraints in the vital infrastructural sectors of power, railways, ports, roads, telecommunications, water, and waste disposal. Shortages and inefficiencies in these sectors are especially damaging to growth, as these are necessary inputs for all other activities in the economy. In some countries of the region in the 1980s, there may have been a shortfall of investment of as much as 2 to 3 percent of

*In some countries of the region in the 1980s, there may have been a shortfall of investment in infrastructure of as much as 2 to 3 percent of GDP.*

GDP, compounded by poor management of existing capacities and inefficient pricing of resources.

In *China* infrastructural constraints are serious. Investment in transport, telecommunications, and energy has lagged behind that in industry. The link between the key sectors of transport and energy is especially close—transporting coal, which accounts for 70 percent of China's power generation, takes up a third of all railway freight capacity, and railways are the dominant mode of transport. In 1989 railway freight was estimated to constitute about 80 percent of the cost of coal delivered to the power sector. There are chronic shortages in transport services in the Chinese economy. The results: electric power shortages (due to the lack of coal transport capacity) and little integration of markets, reducing efficiency. Inadequate communications infrastructure has also hindered the integration of the domestic market.

The ill effects of underinvestment in infrastructure have been compounded with technological backwardness and distortions of consumption patterns resulting from subeconomic pricing of transport services and transport-intensive resources. For example, despite large tariff increases in 1989, long-distance coal transport is still underpriced by as much as 40 percent relative to long-run marginal costs, generating uneconomic demands and congestion. For energy, although free-market coal prices have risen rapidly in the past five years, the administered price is still below domestic supply costs. Electricity tariffs have not provided realistic incentives for producers or consumers until recently. However, recent reforms under the "new plant, new price" policy have resulted in major tariff increases, and it is expected that by the mid-1990s the average level of tariffs will be close to long-run marginal costs.

In the *Philippines* the economic crisis of the early 1980s led to a drastic fall in public and private investment in infrastructure. Some public sector corporations are close to insolvency, and in the power sector, recent pricing policy has been inconsistent with the joint objectives of improving the financial solvency of corporations and adjusting to world petroleum markets. Along with pricing reform, there has to be a significant increase in investment in infrastructure. Bank estimates for 1978–83 show that 4.7 percent of GDP was assigned to infrastructure investment (of which 1.1 percent is attributed to the Bataan Nuclear

Plant alone); this figure fell to 2.6 percent of GDP in 1983–90, with a low of 1.7 percent reached as recently as 1988. Of the public sector's eleven thermal power plants, ten are more than twenty-five years old; maintenance is poor, and more than half have a reliability performance below 50 percent.

Given the fiscal constraints facing the country, greater private sector participation is essential for increasing investment in the power sector. The government has recently announced contracts for five new power plants—to add a projected 1,660 megawatts to total capacity. Even if half of this power comes on stream, it will provide only 20 percent of the increase in power generation needed during the 1990s. In transport, the asset base of the infrastructure has been seriously eroded because of lack of maintenance, poor management, and gross underfunding. The management of existing transport resources must be made more accountable. Local and provincial governments must become involved in handling road networks. And road user charges must be revised to cover costs and mobilize revenues for improving roads.

*Given the fiscal constraints facing the Philippines, greater private sector participation is essential for increasing investment in the power sector.*

In *Indonesia,* despite substantial infrastructure development over successive five-year plans, large unmet demands remain. Only 16 percent of rural households have electricity in Indonesia, and only 30 percent of urban households are connected to municipal water—as against 50 percent or more in comparably developed countries. Quality and efficiency of services remain low in communications and water supply. Pricing infrastructure services to reflect marginal costs of production and aligning petroleum prices with world prices as a means of promoting efficient energy use will be important in rationalizing demand and mobilizing resources for investment, operations, and maintenance.

Urbanization in East Asia is proceeding rapidly, and urban transport problems are particularly serious in the region (box 3.1). In *Thailand* dynamic economic growth in recent years has made infrastructural problems acute, especially in the Bangkok metropolitan area. Investment in the infrastructure averaged 3.5 percent of GDP in the past decade. While urban population grew 3 to 5 percent, real fixed public investment declined steadily between 1985 and 1989—from 7.5 percent of GDP to 3.9 percent, and from 34.7 percent of gross domestic investment to 16.2 percent. The inadequacy of infrastructure was in part a result of limited public investment during the 1980s, reflecting the earlier adjustment strategy that emphasized fiscal caution. By some Bank estimates, Thailand has been underinvesting in infrastructure by 1 to 2 percent of GDP each year over the past decade. That translates, at 1990 levels, to between $800 million and $1.6 billion.

The Bangkok metropolitan region is choking with traffic congestion and air and water pollution. By one Bank estimate, 1.7 percent of the regional GDP is being lost because wage-earners' commuting time to and from the area is so long. Demands for sewerage and water supply in urban areas far exceed the system's present capacity—indicators of inefficient pricing of scarce public resources.

A significant bottleneck in Thailand arises from the institutional side of public finance. Local governments rely on national funding for three-quarters of their projects, and local revenues from property taxes have been inadequate to support the desired level of infrastructure-related services—particularly in Bangkok. Well-designed revenue-sharing schemes are necessary to permit a decentralized system of local public finance to function properly.

In general, infrastructural sectors are characterized by technical or natural monopoly due to economies of scale in production.[7] In such situations, the practice in East Asia and elsewhere in the developing world has been to resort to public sector monopoly. Experience suggests, however, that public sector monopolies have often led to politicization and rent-seeking by interest groups, dispensation of political patronage, poor management of resources, and inefficient pricing of public utilities and factors of production. Alternatives are legislatively regulated private sector monopolies and franchise contracts. An effective regulatory framework is an essential precondition for private sector participation. But private sector industries regulated by government bodies can also result in rent-seeking, political patronage, and barriers to entry and competition. In some situations, it might be preferable to have a well-designed bidding process in which a large number of rival participants can be induced to bid competitively for limited-term public contracts.

East Asian economies—like others in the developing world—have frequently given too little weight to the scarcity value of public resources. The right to use publicly owned resources such as roads and waterways involves the use of scarce resources, and the efficient pricing of such resources generally requires reflecting the opportunity costs of alternative uses. Price signals that reflect the marginal cost of production would promote efficiency in use by allocating available supplies to those valuing them most at the margin. Congestion and excess demand for public utilities are the results of pricing at lower than marginal costs—while excess capacity and wasteful production are the result of an opposite distortion. Better maintenance and better price signals for

**BOX 3.1 URBAN TRANSPORT: SOME WIN-WIN POLICIES**

Increased motorization accompanies economic growth. Motorization rates are still relatively low in Asia, at one car per 67 persons compared with one car per 2.5 persons in OECD countries. But many cities are already congested, and vehicle fleets are growing at about 10 percent a year in several countries, with a heavy concentration in cities. In the absence of improved policies, Asian cities will be dirtier, noisier, and more congested, while they continue to grow rapidly. Better policies—to address negative externalities without discouraging growth—could reduce the urban transport problem at low or no net cost. There are several examples of win-win policies that increase efficiency and have low or even negative public funding costs.

*Economic pricing and taxation.* All means should be considered to achieve congestion pricing and charging for externalities such as pollution. This may require a combination of direct pricing (through taxes on parking spaces and cordon pricing) and space allocation (through decisions on number and location of parking spaces to be provided, on time allowed at metered street parking, on reversible lanes, and so on). Fares for public transport, be it by rail or privately owned road vehicles or publicly owned buses, should cover full costs of infrastructure

public utilities are pressing needs in East Asia. And better price signals would generate more resources to support maintenance, to invest in new capacity, and to provide incentives for the private sector to participate in supplying infrastructural services.

There is also a need for strengthening public bodies to oversee project costs and procurement. Infrastructure investments involve large sums of money, and gestation lags can be long—providing incentives for overpricing. A sudden surge in infrastructure investments could thus lead to inflationary pressures and to large increases in external capital inflows and the risk of debt-service problems. International financial agencies could assist in the scrutiny of projects and pricing policy—for projects they are financing and for the sector as a whole. In fiscal 1992 about 70 percent of the Bank's lending in the region—as against 30 percent for the rest of the Bank—has gone to infrastructure. This orientation will have to continue—with increasing focus on sectoral issues and, as discussed later in this chapter, on environmental concerns in the infrastructural sector.

## Accelerating Enterprise Reform

Enterprise reform is—and will remain for the rest of this decade—an important priority for East Asian countries. This is true for socialist economies in transi-

use and externality taxes. Similarly, appropriate pricing (such as increased diesel prices) can encourage shifts to cleaner fuels.

*Regulations, standards, and public investment.* Air pollution from motorized vehicles is causing increased incidence of illnesses. The poorer urban dwellers are the most exposed and the least able to afford remedies. There is, in addition to proper pricing, a need to:

- Increase standards of fuels and vehicles—unleaded gasolines and low sulfur diesels cost only a cent more per liter than dirtier fuels and yet are rarely available; for motorcycles, two-stroke engines are still allowed even though four-stroke, cleaner engines are available at only a slightly higher cost.
- Increase vehicle inspection for emissions.

*Nonmotorized vehicles* are an efficient use of road space for both personal mobility and freight transport, and they also reduce fuel use and pollution. There is a need to improve attitudes toward walking and bicycling. Among the measures that could help are:

- Providing credit to buy bicycles
- Providing bicycle ways and parking space for bicycles.

An incremental strategy should be followed for mass transit. Busways and segregated lanes might be a good first phase; overpasses and fully elevated busways and light-rail systems might follow.

tion from a centralized command system to a decentralized market system and for other countries with large public sectors and difficult public finance situations. The reform of state-owned enterprises needs to be approached in a pragmatic manner and considered as part of a larger package of enterprise development efforts. These efforts would encompass measures to foster private sector development as well as competition between enterprises (public and private), privatize state enterprises and activities that were previously public monopolies, and strengthen the financial sector's ability to finance increased private sector capital requirements and to lend to public or private enterprises on the basis of commercial criteria, without government guarantees to state enterprises. The emphasis on these three areas will depend on specific circumstances in a given country.

In *China* the current strategy is to reduce the relative role of state enterprises by allowing faster growth in nongovernment-owned enterprises, including joint ventures, rather than by privatizing the enterprises. State enterprises now account for about 55 percent of industrial output and remain a dominant feature of the economy. About a third of them are loss-makers. Their losses accounted for some two-thirds of China's fiscal deficit of about 2.6 percent of GDP in 1991. The overall financing provided to state enterprises is estimated to be a major contributor to the much larger quasi-fiscal deficit, which could be three times as high as the fiscal deficit. Enterprise reform is now a high-priority issue re-

*To fully expose state enterprises in China to hard budget constraints with attendant bankruptcies and unemployment, their 100-million-strong work force needs to be freed from its dependence on the "work unit" for housing, pensions, and income security.*

ceiving attention from the Chinese authorities. For one thing, to fully expose state enterprises to hard budget constraints with attendant bankruptcies and unemployment, their 100-million-strong work force needs to be freed from its dependence on the "work unit" for housing, pensions, and income security. For another, financial authorities and tax collectors ought not to be controlled by the same local authorities that own the enterprises. Complementary actions are also being contemplated. For example, formation of "enterprise groups" through mergers of state enterprises (including financial sector enterprises) that cut across geographical and administrative boundaries is expected to help in creating market competition without privatization. In addition, an outward orientation and joint ownership with foreigners (including financial enterprises) are expected to contribute to market-oriented performance criteria for the state enterprises.

*Viet Nam* is less reliant than China on the state enterprise sector for either output or employment. As a result of reforms to eliminate direct subsidies, some efficiency gains have been made. Industrial distress has also emerged, with the government reluctant to allow many loss-making firms to close for fear of the social consequences. The performance of small and medium-size private firms has been a source of growth. Privatization and other forms of divestiture are now being openly discussed, and experimentation has begun because it is becoming increasingly clear that unlike China, Viet Nam does not have fiscal resources to subsidize the state enterprise sector. Small and medium-size state enterprises absorb more than half of the credit from the banking system—and yet make almost no contribution to the government budget. Privatization is the route to follow for them. But for large enterprises—there are relatively few of them—Viet Nam is likely to draw on the Chinese approach and put emphasis on strengthened management, altered incentives, foreign linkages, and, in some cases, divestiture. As in China, the crucial factor will be the imposition of a hard budget constraint and a willingness to allow liquidation of nonviable state enterprises, while taking steps to permit rapid expansion of private investment.

*Mongolia,* faced with the major shocks of collapse of Soviet aid and of trade with other socialist economies, adopted the more radical approach of privatizing most state enterprises. But because of shortages of spare parts, raw materials, and energy, industrial output has had to be cut back. Moreover, reforms under way, such as price reforms and the conversion of profit remittances to taxes, have reduced old sources of fiscal revenue, while new ones are not yet fully effective. This has led to rapid expansion of money and credit, with consequent inflationary pressures.

---

*In Viet Nam as in China, the crucial factor will be the imposition of a hard budget constraint and a willingness to allow liquidation of nonviable state enterprises, while taking steps to permit rapid expansion of private investment.*

---

In *Cambodia* the authorities accept privatization as an important part of enterprise reform along with a system of greater autonomy for enterprises that remain with the state. The foundation for private development is being established, and informal industry and supporting services have been growing rapidly over the past three years. A problem of sequencing reforms has emerged, however. Enterprise reform combined with price and trade liberalization has slashed the economic rents formerly captured by public sector enterprises through price distortions and budget subsidies. Without appropriate instruments and administration, this revenue loss has not been made up by revenue from the emerging private sector. As a result, budget deficits have increased and essential public expenditures for public investment and operations and maintenance have been reduced.

State-owned enterprises played a relatively modest role in *Malaysia* until the early 1980s. Investment in nonfinancial public enterprises was less than 6 percent of gross investment, much lower than the regional average. But during 1981–85, this ratio shot up to 20 percent. Since then, the government has been trying to reduce the role of state enterprises both by privatization and by reducing the level of investment in state enterprises. In the second half of the 1980s, this investment was reduced to about 14 percent of total investment, and the downward trend is expected to continue. The privatization program launched by the government included partial or total divestment of several government companies, corporatization of selected government departments, and leasing of several government facilities to the private sector. It also provided for management of government-owned installations by private sector management contract and construction of new projects through build-own-operate or build-operate-transfer arrangements and through management buyouts of existing companies or facilities. The government intends to accelerate the pace of privatization, and it is giving particular attention to strengthening the regulatory framework to govern the privatized entities, especially those having monopolistic positions. At the same time, public enterprises will continue to be important in selected strategic and heavy industries—cement, automobiles, petrochemicals, and iron and steel.

In *Thailand* the state enterprise sector accounts for only about 5 percent of GDP and 11 percent of investment—small in comparison with the regional and global averages. Moreover, Thailand has avoided a heavy state presence in manufacturing and trade, and state enterprises are concentrated in power, water, transport, and communications, all sectors in which public ownership is common in most countries. These initial conditions enabled Thailand to follow a gradual approach to privatization and reform of state enterprises. The Thai approach involved putting ceilings on foreign borrowings by the state enterprise sector and encouraging a higher percentage of self-financing for new investments and greater private sector involvement in the financing and management of state enterprises. The accomplishments of these reforms have been impressive in terms of reduced foreign borrowing, lower deficits, and contracting out or leasing of peripheral activities of state enterprises.

*Korea* had a large state sector that accounted for about 40 percent of total investment in the early 1980s. Over the years, that share has been brought down to about 16 percent, and the shares of manufacturing and financial services have been brought down drastically. The government's approach was one of improving state enterprise efficiency through legal and management reforms. A 1989 Bank mission concluded that the efficiency gains due to reforms have been considerable, with significant impact on the profitability of state enterprises.

---

*The bulk of improvement in Indonesia has come from removing constraints on the private sector rather than from privatizing and reforming state enterprises.*

---

In *Indonesia,* where state enterprises play a large role in the economy, improvements have also been gradual, though more modest. The number of state enterprises fell from 221 in 1982 to 211 in 1991, and their share in value added declined from 22 percent to 19 percent. The bulk of improvement has come from removing constraints on the private sector rather than from privatizing and reforming state enterprises. Reforms directed at state enterprises have focused on increasing efficiency rather than privatizing ownership. Deregulation has increased competitive pressures across a range of manufacturing and financial services. Employees of public enterprises are no longer allowed to remain in the civil service. Transfers to public enterprises for new investment have been curtailed, and enterprises are no longer allowed to borrow independently from foreign sources. Efforts have also been made to reduce reliance on the budget by allowing public enterprises greater flexibility in setting prices. A series of decrees from October 1988 through June 1989 established financial soundness indicators—covering profitability, liquidity, and solvency—which are used to rank individual enterprises. Corporate restructuring options that have been proposed range from changing the legal status of an enterprise to liquidation. Complementary changes require that public enterprises prepare five-year corporate plans and annual budgets and work programs for use by management and supervising authorities. Improvements in incentives and accountability are also being fostered by linking salaries to financial performance. Steps are under way to broaden the performance indicators for public enterprises beyond financial measures to encourage greater efficiency.

Profitability of public enterprises has shown some improvement in response to recent reform measures but still remains below potential. For the nonfinancial public sector, the average rate of return on assets is still about 5 percent. Domestic sales prices of major state enterprises remain distorted. Prices of petroleum products and fertilizer in Indonesia are less than half those in Thailand and the Philippines.

In the *Philippines,* despite the strong commitment to a private sector economy, the 1970s witnessed a significant expansion of state enterprises: from 64 in 1970 (including subsidiaries) to 296 in 1988. During 1975–82, investments of state enterprises were about 5 percent of GDP, although they declined to about 2 percent during 1983–90. The government's reform program put emphasis on privatization, with the state enterprises to be retained or merged with others—just 31 percent in number and 40 percent in value of assets—representing a substantial reduction. For retained state enterprises the government has implemented programs of increased financial autonomy and improved management by developing multiyear corporate plans, setting annual performance targets, insulating state enterprises from political intervention, and instilling operating practices akin to those of the private sector.

This review of state enterprise reform programs by East Asian countries over the past decade illustrates the diversity of approaches followed by these countries. Common issues deserving further attention include:

- The need to establish and enforce hard budget constraints for state enterprises

- The establishment of efficient and socially acceptable mechanisms to close down loss-making enterprises (whether public or private), including bankruptcy procedures

- The reform of financial sector institutions that might be required to support an expanding private sector and an increasingly independent and accountable state enterprise sector

- The introduction of competition in sectors that were formerly public monopolies, and, in general, greater competition at the enterprise level through removal of barriers to entry and exit

- A greater place for private participation, whether through outright divestiture, build-operate-transfer arrangements, leases, management contracts, or other privatization instruments.

## Continuing Financial Sector Reforms

A related and important issue is reform of the financial sector. In the interventionist era of 1965–80, many East Asian market economies had negative real interest rates and financial repression. In the 1980s many of these economies launched some program of financial liberalization. The passage has been rough, but those that achieved some success did so by modifying the reform strategy to suit the requirements of their economies.

Korea started its financial reform in 1981–82, Malaysia toward the end of 1978, the Philippines in 1980, and Indonesia in 1983. Although motivations varied according to circumstances, reform came when authorities realized that the interventionist regime was inefficient and ineffective—particularly when macroeconomic imbalances were stark and unsettling. Financial liberalization policies, although diverse, had similar goals, such as the attainment of positive real interest rates and enhanced competitiveness of the financial systems. But the degree of success varied among countries, depending on whether they were able to maintain macroeconomic stability and steadfastness in continuing the pace of reforms.

The macroeconomic environment in *Korea* in the second half of the 1980s was propitious for the initiation of financial liberalization. With a favorable turn in its terms of trade, a stable inflation rate, appreciation of the real exchange rate,

*In the 1980s many of these economies launched some program of financial liberalization. The passage has been rough, but those that achieved some success did so by modifying the reform strategy to suit the requirements of their economies.*

and restrained monetary policy, Korea adopted a strategy of introducing new financial products with relatively high interest rates that moved closely with market rates, rather than deregulating the rates on existing products. The band system for bank lending rates was introduced and further widened. A certificate of deposit was introduced with a market-determined interest rate. Entry barriers to the banking sector were lowered after the denationalization of the nationwide commercial banks, and the entry of foreign banks was sanctioned. Real interest rates turned positive because of the upward adjustment in ceilings on interest rates and because of the reduced inflation rate. But this period also witnessed the ballooning of nonperforming bank loans, and the government had to intervene partly to protect the solvency of the banking system. This and the high leveraging of Korean firms stymied efforts at interest rate deregulation.

In December 1988 the government took major steps toward more effective deregulation of interest rates. Most bank and nonbank lending rates and some long-term lending rates were decontrolled except on some policy loans and short-term deposit rates (for fear of excessive competition among financial intermediaries). The government reversed this policy soon after, however, and interest rates tended to become more rigid. In November 1991 the government began a long-term plan to fully deregulate the interest rate structure by 1997.

In *Malaysia* financial institutions initially operated under more competitive conditions than did those in other East Asian countries. The operations and management of commercial banks—including government-owned commercial banks—were largely autonomous, and there was considerable freedom of entry of new banks and branch expansion. Malaysia also had a relatively large securities market. Although Malaysia had an administered system of interest rates, there was a wide range of financial instruments with interest rates determined by market conditions. Interest rate controls had been retained mainly to ensure the stability of domestic interest rates within a system with an open capital account and floating exchange rate and to promote the indigenous banks by limiting price competition with dominant foreign banks.

Interest rate deregulation, which permitted commercial banks to determine their own interest rates, thus meant a small change in the Malaysian financial system. In addition, in Malaysia's stable macroeconomic environment, full financial liberalization could succeed without untoward consequences. Malaysia did, however, face the serious problem of nonperforming loans, but this was overcome with relative ease because of well-administered supervisory arrangements and effective prudential control.

The *Philippines'* financial liberalization coincided with the emergence of severe macroeconomic imbalances. The balance of payments and fiscal deficits were large and persistent and the inflation rate and interest rates were high, exposing the underlying structural weakness of the economy. Financial liberalization policy took various forms. Banking laws were amended in 1980 to permit the adoption of universal banking. To facilitate the change, the ceilings on deposit rates and on various categories of bank lending were relaxed and then removed. The last remnants of controls on interest rates—on deposits with a maturity of two years or less and on short-term loans—were eliminated by 1984. The interest rate subsidy on preferential credits was abolished in 1985. Banks that became unibanks were required to broaden their ownership base so that no one family or business could retain control.

During the initial years of financial liberalization, 1980–84, developments in the financial sector reflected progress toward the intended goals. Real interest rates were positive, mainly because of decelerated inflation immediately after the reforms. After 1984, there was an upsurge in both nominal and real interest rates, which, because of their adverse impact on highly leveraged corporate borrowers, accounted for the large and growing volume of nonperforming bank loans. The government had to bail out some banks and take over others. But by 1990 the direct role of the government in commercial banking declined dramatically with the shrinkage of Philippine National Bank. The profitability of the banking system improved markedly, as did the capital and retained earnings of the system. But the balance sheet of the Central Bank of the Philippines suffered as a result.

*Indonesia* undertook financial liberalization as part of its efforts to restructure the economy following the oil-price shock of the 1980s. In the early phases of reform, the government deregulated interest rates of commercial banks, replaced credit ceilings with a system of reserve money management, and adjusted interest rates on a simplified structure of directed subsidized credit. Between 1984 and 1985, new money market instruments were introduced along with a rediscount window at Bank Indonesia to strengthen control of monetary policies. The authorities introduced additional reforms in 1988–89: restrictions on entry and branching by foreign and domestic banks were lessened, and banks and nonbank financial intermediaries were allowed to issue certificates of deposit and to raise capital in the stock market.

In 1990, the government reduced the size and scope of subsidized directed credit programs and again raised interest rates on those that remained. Since the emphasis of reforms was on credit evaluation and the proper pricing of loans and on financial management of assets based on profitability, a better environ-

*The Indonesian financial system responded well to liberalization, achieving positive real interest rates and higher growth and greater diversity of the financial system.*

ment was created for the financial sector. The Indonesian financial system responded well to liberalization, achieving positive real interest rates and higher growth and greater diversity of the financial system.

But Indonesia's progress on financial liberalization was complicated by attempts to lower domestic rates and by a boom in investment demand, both of which put pressures on the balance of payments. The government's subsequent tight monetary policy has kept interest rates high and increased levels of nonperforming loans. The government has responded by strengthening the banking system through more effective supervision and by tightening fiscal policy, thereby creating room for lower interest rates without endangering external balance.

Reforming the financial sector has high payoffs and deserves to be high on the policy agenda. As East Asian countries continue to address the unfinished agenda on financial sector reforms, they will need to draw lessons from their rich experience in the sequencing and methods of financial liberalization.

First, it is important that the approach to interest rate policy and financial sector liberalization take into account the existing financial position of the private sector and the quality of prudential regulation of the financial system. If the macroeconomic environment is unstable and bank supervision is ineffective, interest rate liberalization ought to be gradual to avoid possible disruptions to long-standing financial practices that can emerge from a sudden removal of interest rate regulations. The importance of strong banking regulations and supervisory policy needs to be underscored, not only because they ensure the

*Reforming the financial sector has high payoffs and deserves to be high on the policy agenda.*

viability and health of the banking industry, which is their traditional microeconomic justification, but also because interest rate liberalization would be ineffectual without them.

Second, institutional change should be in the forefront of financial sector reforms. This includes establishing a strong supporting infrastructure that will provide for adequate information flow, credit appraisal and rating, and legal and accounting systems and for the development of equity markets. Such institutional reforms will help reduce the dependence of firms on bank credit and orient them toward equity financing. Firms' vulnerability to interest rate shocks would then be attenuated, allowing greater scope for full-scale interest rate liberalization at later stages.

Third, interest rate strategies must be tailored according to whether inflation is low or unacceptably high. A gradual program of interest rate liberalization that maintains positive real rates will be effective in low-inflation countries, if banking supervision is strong and effectively enforced and if demand management and other policies are in place to maintain economic stability. Within that group, countries with relatively long periods of price stability achieved through sound and credible macroeconomic policies are good candidates for full interest rate liberalization subject to a strengthened system of prudential regulations over the banking system. In high-inflation countries, a strong and credible stabilization program and an equally strong set of prudential regulations are generally the best initial policy measures, followed by interest rate deregulation when the monetary situation has been stabilized and banking supervision strengthened.

## Stepping Up Environmental Protection

*World Development Report 1992* (World Bank 1992e) highlighted the link between growth and environment. In addition to achieving rapid income growth, East Asian countries have made progress in many environmentally important areas, including rural sanitation and availability of drinking water. The region's accumulated problems, however, in some respects are about the worst among the developing regions. These are in the areas of soil erosion, waterlogging, and salinization; urban environmental degradation; industrial pollution and energy sector emissions; and deforestation and loss of habitat.

Soil degradation, widespread throughout East Asia, has multiple causes: erosion, waterlogging, salinization, and overgrazing. Soil degradation has led to significant reductions in cultivable land and pressure on remaining natural habitats as farmers continue to seek marginal lands. Although national-level data are not readily available, the extent of land degradation in Asia (20 percent of all vegetated land) exceeds the world average (17 percent). In addition, the suspended load per square kilometer of drainage basin in Asia, as an indication of soil erosion, is three to eight times the world average.

Rapid population growth and urbanization in Asia, combined with inadequate infrastructure, are leading to increasing environmental degradation in urban areas. Water pollution, caused by both untreated sewage and industrial effluents, is perhaps the most serious problem for health. Governments have typically focused on water supply rather than on sanitation or sewage treatment. In most Asian cities, adequate sewerage infrastructure is available only in the more affluent neighborhoods, and virtually no sewage is treated. Data from the U.N. Global Environmental Monitoring System show that levels of fecal coliform and dissolved mercury in Asian rivers exceed the recommended levels by

50 to 100 times. Although lead levels in Asian rivers are generally within safe levels, other toxic wastes have contaminated the heavily fished coastal waters of China, Indonesia, and Thailand. Finally, groundwater resources, often used for urban supplies, are being rapidly depleted by overuse and contaminated by seepage of surface pollutants. Jakarta has so overused its groundwater that salt water has now contaminated shallow wells in a 5-to-10-kilometer-wide belt along the coast.

Asian cities also have high levels of air pollutants that threaten human health, including particulate matter, lead, carbon monoxide, sulfur dioxide, ozone, and nitrogen oxide. World Health Organization (WHO) data show that nine of the fifteen cities with the highest particulate levels are East Asian:[8] and six of the fifteen cities with the highest sulfur dioxide levels are East Asian.[9] Ambient levels of particulate matter exceed WHO standards 100 days or more each year in Jakarta, Bangkok, and China's larger cities—compared with less than ten days in most developed countries. Similarly, sulfur dioxide air pollution exceeds WHO standards more than 50 days a year in some East Asian cities—among the highest measures anywhere. In all cities, motor vehicles account for much of the air pollution, and the number of cars is growing at an astounding rate. Vehicle registration in the greater Bangkok metropolitan area grew by 40 percent in 1990 alone. Elsewhere, the number of motor vehicles is growing by 10 percent or more a year, and doubling every seven years.

---

*In East Asia carbon dioxide emissions per unit of GDP are three times the level in Latin America, and energy used per unit of GDP is nearly double.*

---

In East Asia carbon dioxide emissions per unit of GDP are three times the level in Latin America, and energy used per unit of GDP is nearly double (figure 3.1). Technologies, product mix, energy pricing, and conservation practices have all contributed to the situation. Things could get worse. If past trends continue, East Asia will account for more than half of the world's incremental carbon dioxide and sulfur dioxide, except to the extent that cleaner technologies are used. China emits 16 times the amount of sulfur dioxide that Japan does (18 million tons, compared with 1.1 million tons), and this could increase by 50 to 100 percent in the next twenty years. Thailand spews out 3 million tons of sulfur dioxide.

Throughout East Asia, accelerating natural resource degradation, especially deforestation, is threatening the region's biodiversity. Each year, East Asia

FIGURE 3.1 ENVIRONMENTAL INDICATORS

***East Asia achieved high efficiency in labor and capital use, but its environmental record is poor.***

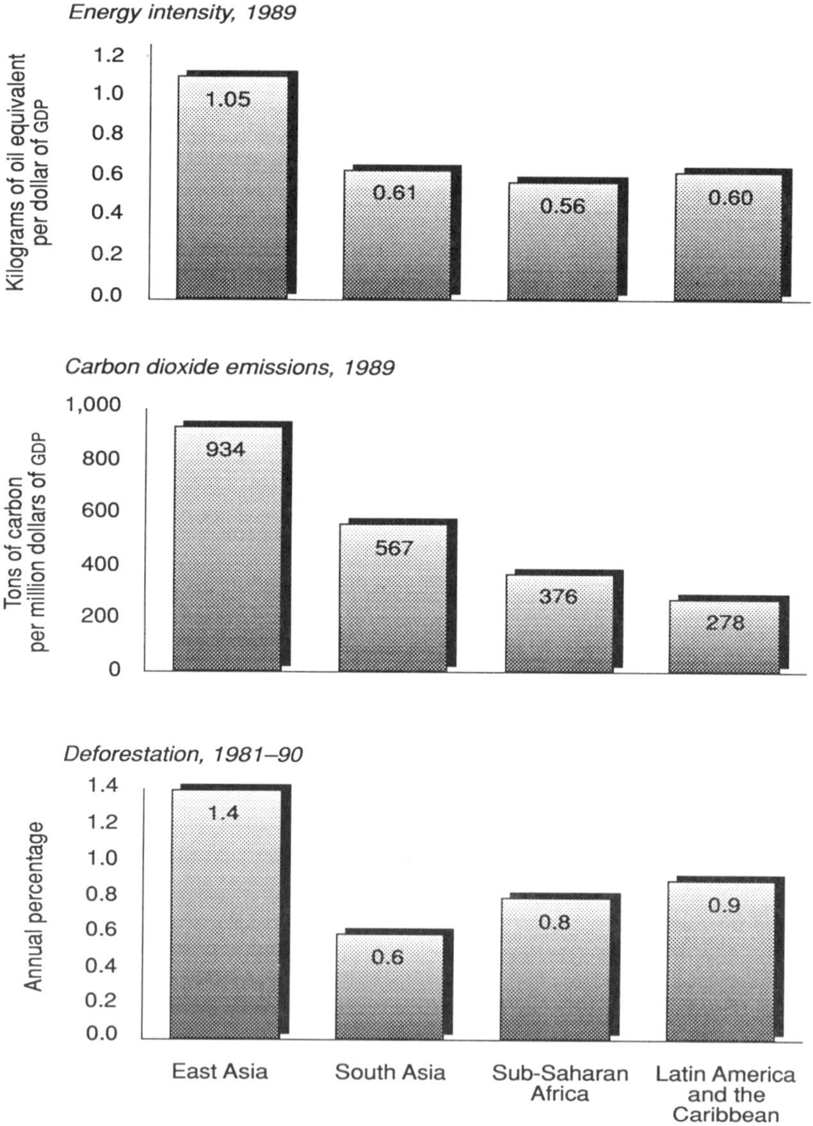


*Source:* World Bank 1992e; World Resources Institute 1992; World Bank staff estimates.

(excluding China) loses nearly 2 million hectares of forest—0.7 percent of the total. In the 1980s deforestation in East Asia was higher than in any other region of the developing world (see figure 3.1). Deforestation is particularly high in Myanmar, Lao P.D.R., and Cambodia, where national control has broken down and loggers are indiscriminately exploiting resources with the tacit help of regional neighbors.

*Each year, East Asia (excluding China) loses nearly 2 million hectares of forest—0.7 percent of the total.*

In East Asia, as elsewhere, there is growing recognition that environmental degradation carries a price in health costs and mortality and loss of productivity and output in resource-based sectors. Political commitment to protecting the environment is also increasing. Almost all East Asian countries have legislated protection of their air, land, and water. Many have created environmental ministries or specialized agencies. Some have (or are drawing up) guidelines and standards to enforce the legislation.

There are several areas of agreement in East Asia on how best to approach environmental protection. First, it is easier to control degradation in a growing economy than in a stagnant one. So, slower growth is not the best way to reduce industrial and urban pollution. Second, punitive regulation alone will be less effective than a collaborative effort in which industry actively sets standards and guidelines, monitors itself, and establishes fair and efficient enforcement systems. Nongovernmental organizations have an important role to play in this area. Third, attention to the costs and benefits of specific environmental issues is important for project appraisal and policy analysis.

Many countries are taking action on pricing, taxation, and regulatory policies—in addition to a program of environmental investment. In the urban sector, for example, multipronged approaches to vehicle congestion and air pollution are being increasingly incorporated in East Asia (China, Indonesia, Korea, the Philippines, and Thailand). These include taxes aimed at vehicles, fuels, parking, or road use; traffic management, land management, and aggressive vehicle inspection; and programs to upgrade technologies and fuels, such as unleaded gasoline (as in Bangkok), and to reduce the number of diesel and two-stroke engines in urban fleets. In residential areas, fuel switching (say, from coal to natural gas, as in Seoul) and fuel upgrading are priorities. In industry, strategies to deal with pollution aim at combining incentives (tax rebates, loans, accelerated depreciation, lower tariffs) with sanctions (fines, user charges, and direct intervention). There is promise, too, in collective solutions: collective treatment

*Although environmental programs in East Asia are moving in the right direction, the pace of progress is too slow.*

at industrial estates or private sector pretreatment before disposal into public sewers, especially for such industries as tanning, dyes, and electronics.

Although environmental programs are moving in the right direction, the pace of progress is too slow, for several reasons:

- The political will and governance needed to tackle environmental problems are lacking in many places.

- Price distortions still cause substantial inefficiencies and excessive resource use in many places. Economic reform is an essential complement to environmental regulation.

FIGURE 3.2 INCREMENTAL CARBON DIOXIDE EMISSIONS, 1990–2000

***East Asia's increase in carbon dioxide emissions in the 1990s will be larger than that of the rest of the world together.***

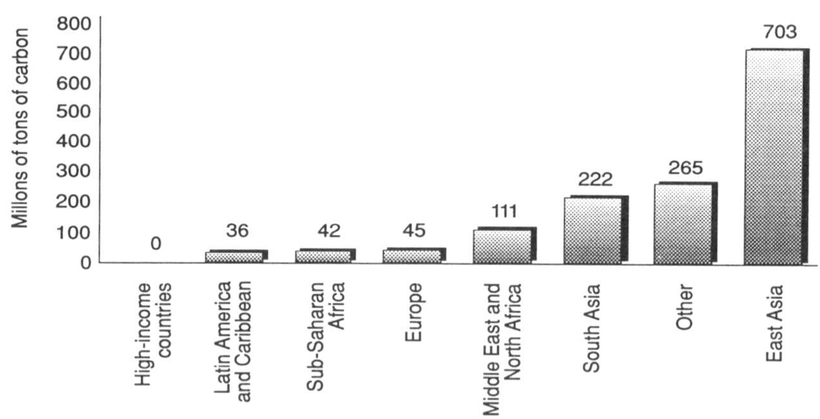


*Note:* Incremental carbon dioxide emissions from high-income countries are held at zero, according to the ceiling set at the United Nations Conference on Environment and Development.
*Source:* World Bank 1992e; World Bank staff estimates.

■ Additional resources needed to address environmental problems in East Asia are estimated to be as much as $20 billion a year by the end of the century (World Bank 1992e). Most East Asian companies that devote a high percentage of income to development might not be able to finance these additional costs from domestic sources. Additional external resources will be needed.

■ There is a lack of consensus about the serious global consequences of environmental degradation in East Asia. For example, a 20 percent reduction in annual carbon dioxide emission (currently 2,700 million tons) in all the industrial countries will be offset by emissions in East Asia within ten years (figure 3.2). Forests and other habitats in East Asia are more threatened by population and industrial expansion than in any other region. Yet the countries most affected by deforestation (for example, Indonesia and Malaysia) see that a global agreement, balancing national and world interests, has not been developed.

The environment, then, poses a major challenge to East Asia and the global community, with inadequate programs in place or in sight. Future environmental work in Asia will rely on increased official financial flows, increased direct private sector investment, new technology, local participation, and renewed emphasis on the policy and institutional regimes in which environmental concerns are evaluated, monitored, and regulated. There is a need for an environmental initiative in East Asia to develop a consensus on programs and policies and to mobilize resources, domestic and external, to fund these programs.

CHAPTER FOUR

# Global Perspectives and Regional Priorities

EAST Asia has shown remarkable resilience to external shocks, but this does not mean that the external environment is irrelevant for the region. On the contrary, in view of its greater global links, external factors are all the more important. But East Asia's experience emphasizes the value of vigilance, pragmatism, and flexibility in responding to the changing external environment—the same attributes that will be needed in the 1990s, not only for the success stories to be sustained but for other East Asian countries to join in the process.

## Global Economic Growth

The outlook for the global economy is sluggish, and world economic growth is likely to be relatively modest in 1992 and 1993. With recession in the United States and the collapse of output in Eastern Europe and the former Soviet Union, global output per capita declined in 1991 for the first time since 1982—by about 1 percent—and the decline was expected to continue in 1992. There might be some growth in 1993, but the recovery will be less robust than in earlier recovery years (1988, 1984, 1976).

The economies in all of the major industrial countries are growing at quite similar rates—about 2 percent a year. This convergence to modest performance reflects the sluggish recovery in the United States, the significant slowdown in Japan, and the relatively poor performance in Europe, including Germany. In Europe, the situation is particularly uncertain and fragile—with some volatility in exchange markets and interest rates and a lack of clarity about the future directions of European union. In the United States, export growth has slowed. A weakened financial system and the lack of consumer and business confidence mean that, despite lower interest rates, the recovery is likely to be slow. Certainly, there is nothing to suggest that the traditional recovery rate of 4 to 5 percent a year will be achieved any time soon. Nor is the outlook very bright in the near term for Japan, the most important partner for East Asia (box 4.1). The recent decline in stock prices in Japan exceeded in real terms the decline in the U.S. stock market following the crash of 1929. The recent move of the Japanese authorities to provide significant fiscal stimulus is a welcome development, but GDP is likely to grow at less than 3 percent a year in Japan in 1992 and 1993.

Underlying these short-term developments is the long-term trend in productivity growth in the industrial countries, about 1.5 percentage points less than it was before 1973 (figure 4.1). In fact, productivity growth was slower in the 1980s than in the 1970s, despite the decline in oil prices, disinflation, and structural reform. This feature is also shared by all developing regions outside Asia. Thus, regardless of the strength or weakness of short-term performance, the underlying growth of potential output in the world economy is now slower than it has been in the past.

The sluggish outlook on growth in the industrial countries is cause for concern because of the observed association between the growth of per capita GDP in industrial and developing countries (figure 4.2). In the past, East Asia has managed to escape this association. But if the relationship holds in the aggregate for the developing countries and if other regions improve their performance, East Asia might face difficulties in sustaining its past record. Efforts must thus be made not only to improve the growth rates in industrial countries but also to increase their impact on growth rates in developing countries. Among the measures that can help the second objective are increasing developing country penetration of industrial country markets and increasing trade among developing countries.

## Trade and Investment

Imports of manufactures from developing countries form a very small share (barely 3 percent) of consumption in industrial countries (table 4.1). With the globalization of technology and capital flows, comparative advantage in many manufactures is shifting to the developing countries. If the developing countries follow outward-oriented policies and the industrial countries maintain open trading systems, exports of manufactures from developing countries can increase substantially during the 1990s and beyond. And if so, East Asia can sustain its rapid development along with other successfully developing regions.

It is in this context that the growing protectionism in industrial countries is of serious concern to East Asia and other developing regions. It has been estimated that if protection in the European Community (EC), Japan, and the United States were halved, developing-country exports could rise by about $50 billion in 1988 prices (World Bank 1992c). East Asia would benefit the most, accounting for more than half the increase. By the same token, East Asia would be the most seriously affected if industrial-country protection rose. The stalling of the GATT's Uruguay Round, the increased trade friction among the EC, Japan, and the United States, and now the accelerating trend toward regional trading arrangements are worrying developments for East Asia.

The creation of the EC single market, for example, could hit East Asia's larger exporters of manufactures—even if the EC's common external trade barriers do not rise. The reason: trade creation in the EC after 1992, although high (assuming higher EC growth and high income elasticity for manufactures), would be eclipsed by even higher trade diversion. The EC's estimates indicate that imports would fall by about 10 percent as a result of the reforms—2.5

---

**BOX 4.1 GROWING CENTRALITY OF JAPAN IN EAST ASIAN ECONOMIES: A QUIET TRANSFORMATION**

Without much fanfare, Japan is quietly replacing the United States as the key partner in the development of East Asia—in aid, trade, and foreign direct investment. Lately, this has expanded to include financial flows and economic policy advice, as well as portfolio investment.

Of official development assistance commitments of about $10.6 billion to East Asia from all sources, about half came from Japan and only 6 percent or so from the United States. Similarly, of total net foreign direct investment to East Asia in 1990, Japan's share was 30 percent, and the U.S. share only 10 percent.

In trade, Japan is becoming the principal source of imports to East Asian countries, while the United States remains the principal market for East Asian goods. In 1990, East Asian imports from Japan were about $79 billion, exports to Japan about $53 billion. Their trade deficit with Japan was more than matched by their trade surplus with the United States, which imported about $82 billion from East Asia but could export only about $53 billion. For Japan, exports to East Asia constitute about 30 percent of total exports and have been growing in current dollars at about 13 percent a year from 1984 to 1990; Japan's exports to the United States are at about the same level but are growing much more slowly.

East Asia's trade patterns are powerfully influenced by Japanese direct investment flows, which have been growing rapidly during the past five

percent from removing internal barriers to trade and a further 7.5 percent from removing cost-raising regulatory barriers. The greatest trade diversion would be in services and technology-intensive manufactures, so the immediate effect on East Asia would not be significant. But trade diversion could also be large for labor-intensive manufactures. The removal of internal trade and regulatory barriers within the EC could increase the competitiveness of exporters of labor-intensive manufactures within the EC—particularly in Greece, Portugal, and Spain. And this could have significant implications for East Asian exports in the short term.

East Asia is concerned also with the possible implications of the North American Free Trade Agreement (NAFTA) among Canada, Mexico, and the United States. The major concern is the impact of rules of origin affecting textiles, automobiles, and electronic goods. There is also concern that some potential flows of capital to developing East Asia might be diverted.

---

years. Whereas Japanese company affiliates in North America and in Europe are designed primarily to supply local markets, those in Asia export a large part of their production to markets around the world, particularly markets in East Asia. Japanese direct investments in East Asia are being increasingly supplemented by portfolio investments, not only in Hong Kong and Singapore but also in stock markets in Indonesia, Malaysia, and Thailand. The Japanese companies are also being encouraged to list their shares on local stock markets, so as to raise money more cheaply than on the depressed Tokyo market.

There is also a new phenomenon in the development of Japanese economic and financial integration with East Asia: policy advice from Tokyo to Asian capitals. In 1990, the Bank of Japan surveyed the financial systems of members of the Association of South East Asian Nations (ASEAN) and the Asian newly industrialized economies and made various policy recommendations, which included a warning against the removal of exchange controls before the domestic savings base is large enough to support local development without recourse to excessive external financing.

Japan's systems of financial intermediation and industrial organization are of growing interest to other developing countries, particularly in Asia. Japan's own success has relied on multilateralism and an open global economic system. Japanese trade surpluses can be good news for development, provided they are associated with resource transfers to developing countries, including those in East Asia.

FIGURE 4.1 PRODUCTIVITY GROWTH IN THE OECD, 1964–92
(real GDP per employee)

***A slowdown in productivity growth in OECD countries does not augur well for their growth prospects.***

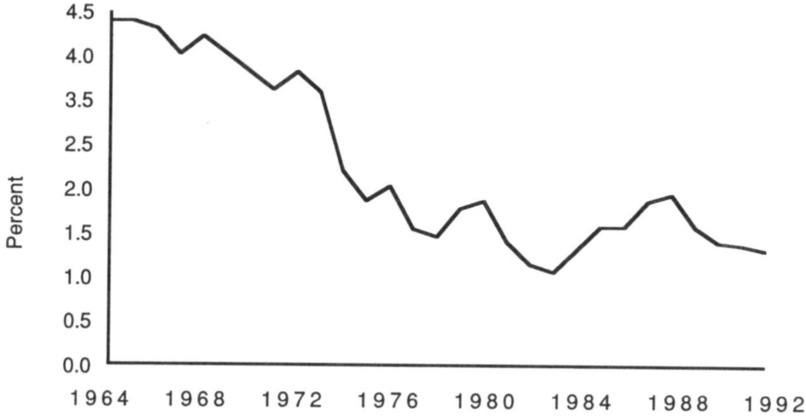


*Source:* World Bank staff estimates.

FIGURE 4.2 GROWTH IN PER CAPITA GDP IN INDUSTRIAL AND DEVELOPING COUNTRIES, 1965–93

***The sluggish growth outlook for industrial countries is cause for serious concern for developing countries.***

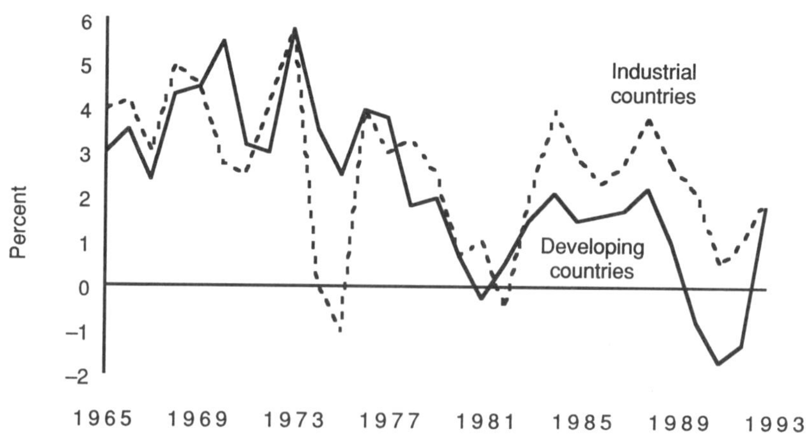


*Source:* World Bank staff estimates.

The longer-term effect of regionalism on East Asia's trade prospects will depend crucially on whether regional trading blocs help—or hinder—global multilateral trade liberalization. If trade barriers decline, the benefits are enormous. But if trade barriers rise or trade frictions escalate, one of the principal casualties in terms of lower growth and lost opportunities would be the open economies of East Asia. East Asians are concerned about tendencies to regionalism in world trade.

Should East Asia, then, form a regional trading bloc to counter the challenge from other blocs? The arguments for such an initiative are weak. The regimes in East Asia range from virtually free trade in Hong Kong and Singapore to the more restrictive import regime of China. A formal free trade area would pose serious administrative and economic difficulties. Moreover, a free trade area requires some harmonization of fiscal, monetary, and exchange rate policies among the partners—a difficult, if not impossible, goal given the vast differences of political and economic systems in East Asia. Perhaps most important, the impressive performance of trade and foreign investment in East Asia in the 1980s flies in the face of the argument that a large internal market is necessary for developing exports, for attracting foreign direct investment, or for exploiting economies of scale. Singapore, for example, with a population of less than 3 million, exports about $35 billion worth of manufactures a year—about twice as much as Brazil, which has a population of 150 million. A trading bloc would more likely foster an inward orientation, impairing the worldwide search for market opportunities that has served East Asia so well.

East Asia must, by contrast, continue to press for multilateralism and consistency of regional blocs with the GATT—not only in words but also in spirit. If

TABLE 4.1 IMPORTS FROM DEVELOPING COUNTRIES AS A SHARE OF CONSUMPTION (percent)

***Open trade policies allow developing countries to substantially increase exports of manufactures.***

| *Item* | *1968* | *1974* | *1980* | *1984* | *1988* |
|---|---|---|---|---|---|
| EC [a] | 1.1 | 1.7 | 2.7 | 2.9 | 2.9 |
| North America | 0.8 | 1.8 | 2.4 | 3.1 | 4.1 |
| Japan | 0.9 | 1.7 | 1.7 | 1.7 | 1.8 |
| Total | 0.9 | 1.7 | 2.4 | 2.9 | 3.1 |

*Note:* Data are for all manufactures.
a. Membership of the EC grew from six to twelve during this period.
*Source:* United Nations Conference on Trade and Development.

*A trading bloc would more likely foster an inward orientation, impairing the worldwide search for market opportunities that has served East Asia so well.*

Europe and North America do not violate the spirit of multilateralism, East Asia has the ability—and responsibility—to further promote multilateral trading in the region, as the United States did over the past thirty years. Concerted regionwide actions in trade and investment, as opposed to the establishment of a regional bloc, could promote greater openness—even when regionally coordinated—by being nondiscriminatory and global. Such reforms are likely to proceed faster, be less easily reversible, and be more effective. Simultaneous trade liberalizations create demand for each other's products and thus promote exports and income more than would unilateral trade liberalizations. They are also less prone to reversals than unilateral trade reforms.

The GATT process is a good starting point. Regionwide actions are consistent with—and complementary to—trade liberalization and can carry it farther, discouraging discriminatory trading blocs. As with earlier GATT negotiations among industrial countries, East Asia has a manageable number of countries with strong complementarities to make concerted trade liberalization mutually beneficial. The East Asian countries are also strong enough to take the lead in multilateral liberalization and to provide benefits (such as most-favored-nation concessions) to other developing countries. All this, of course, is contingent on having other parts of the world abide by the rules of an open trade system.

In promoting trade within East Asia, the region can build on its own style of promoting regional integration. That integration has been taking place in the framework of markets with little institutional structure. Intraregional trade expansion is particularly remarkable in the golden triangle of Southeast Asia (consisting of parts of Indonesia, Malaysia, and Singapore), in the South China Zone (Hong Kong, Taiwan [China], and the southern provinces of China), and in the Yellow Sea area (Japan, Korea, and the northeastern provinces of China). Integration has taken a new turn with increased intraindustry and intrafirm cooperation. More and more, products undergo different stages in production in different countries in the region, capitalizing on their comparative advantages. In this East Asian style of regional integration, foreign direct investment is leading the way, followed by export promotion and import liberalization, thus creating jobs and output in new sectors before competition throws workers out of employment in old inefficient sectors.

Thus in the 1980s, East Asia's international economic linkages through trade were shaped, in part, by big increases in foreign direct investment. In the 1970s, East Asia accounted for about 16 percent of total foreign direct investment flows to developing countries. In the 1980s, its share more than doubled (figure 4.3). Part of the reason was China's emergence as an attractive home for foreign capital: wages in coastal China are only 20 percent of the average wage in Hong Kong and 70 percent of that in Malaysia; the average cost of factory construction in Hong Kong is more than five times that in Zhuhai, a special economic zone in Guangdong Province.

Japanese foreign direct investment grew sharply in the 1980s, accounting for between a third and a half of all such flows to East Asia. More recently, the newly industrialized economies of Hong Kong, Korea, Singapore, and Taiwan (China) have become the biggest foreign investors in China, Indonesia, and Malaysia (figure 4.4).

There is thus much potential in concerted action to provide foreign direct investment in Asia. Hong Kong, Japan, Korea, Singapore, and Taiwan (China) are emerging as major sources of investment in the region's developing economies, where a rapid increase in foreign investment is a key issue for reform

FIGURE 4.3 SHARES OF FOREIGN DIRECT INVESTMENT TO DEVELOPING COUNTRIES (percent)

***East Asia's share of total foreign direct investment to developing countries doubled***

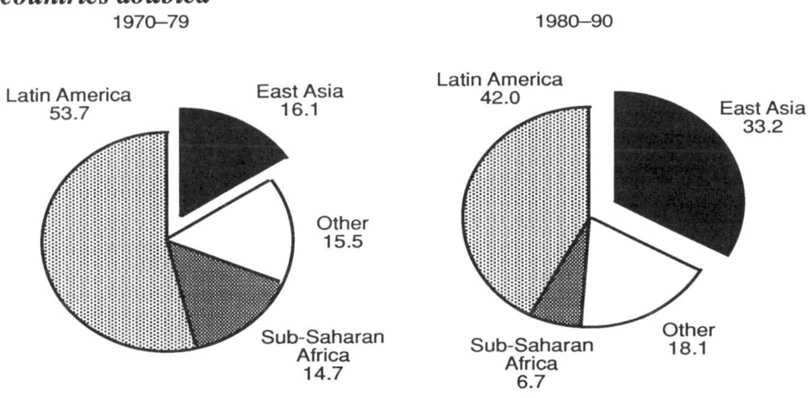


*Source:* World Bank staff estimates.

FIGURE 4.4 SHARE OF INWARD NET FLOWS OF FOREIGN DIRECT INVESTMENT, LATE 1980S

***Japan and the newly industrialized economies are displacing the United States and the EC as the dominant sources of foreign investment.***

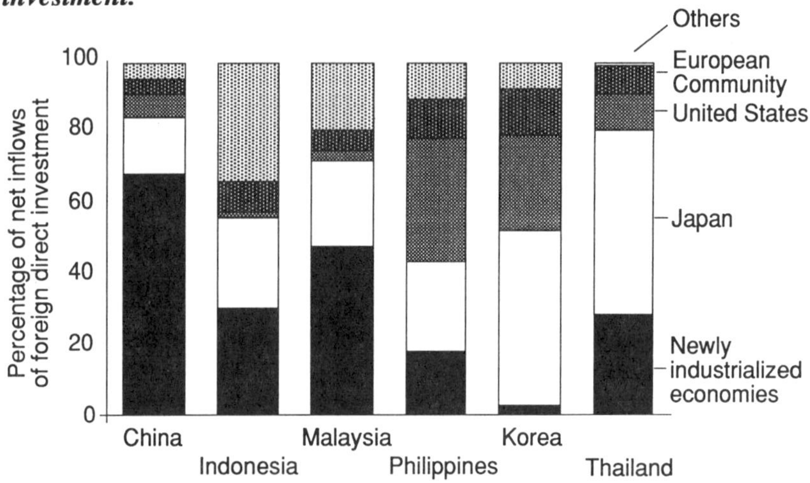


*Source:* UNCTC 1991.

and growth. Harmonizing the policies for foreign direct investment and finding ways of stimulating it are thus likely to be at the cutting edge of regional integration in East Asia.

## External Capital Flows

Foreign direct investment will be a key component of increased external capital inflows in East Asia during the 1990s. As noted in chapter 1, current account deficits of the region were less than 1 percent of the regional GDP during 1965–90. But that figure rose to about 2 percent in 1991 and is forecast to rise further during the 1990s. The resource requirements for reforms in socialist economies in transition are likely to be substantial, as are the investment requirements for infrastructural development and environmental protection in the region. Estimates of the external resource requirements for the region depend strongly on the resource gaps of China, which have fluctuated widely in recent years (a switch of $17 billion in current account balance between 1989 and 1990). At this point, external resource requirements for the region (excluding Korea) by the mid-1990s are estimated at about 3 percent of GDP, or $30 billion (at 1990 prices), a year.

This is taking place in an environment of improving resource flows to developing countries. Slower growth in the United States has been associated with lower interest rates and smaller current account deficits. This has been combined with an increasing current account surplus in Japan. The current account deficits of the high-income countries, unusually large in the 1980s, are coming down. From $70 billion in 1990, they declined to about $11 billion in 1991 and are projected to remain around that level for 1992–93 (table 4.2). This has enabled an increase in resource flows to Europe and the former Soviet Union and to Latin America and the Caribbean. Similar increases in resource flows are occurring for East Asia in the 1990s.

---

*Rapid growth of exports was a key element enabling East Asian countries to tackle their debt problems in the 1980s.*

---

Increasing reliance on external resources will call for continued prudent management of resources in East Asian countries. It is noteworthy that external debt in East Asia grew rapidly—more rapidly than in Latin America—during the 1970s and 1980s. Nevertheless, East Asian countries, except for the Philippines, managed to avoid a debt crisis. Prudent macroeconomic management together with flexible exchange rate management helped them maintain export competitiveness, encourage domestic savings, and discourage capital flight. Rapid growth of exports was a key element enabling East Asian countries to tackle their debt problems in the 1980s. This experience reinforces the need for continued expansion of trade during the 1990s if the region is to meet its external resource requirements without creating a debt problem. That is why an open trading environment is so vital for the region.

Increasing the share of non-debt-creating inflows is another way to contain the debt service burden. A large part of external resource flows for East Asia can, in fact, be expected to be foreign direct investment. Already in 1991, such flows in East Asia were close to $10 billion, and a major increase during the 1990s is a real possibility. A significant part can go to infrastructural development—if, of course, policies in recipient countries are suitably redesigned. However, foreign direct investment also creates contingent liabilities and, to the extent that such flows move in concert, attracting and holding them requires sophistication in macroeconomic management.

Official development finance, both concessional and nonconcessional, will continue to be important. In particular, for the low-income socialist economies

TABLE 4.2 BALANCES ON CURRENT ACCOUNT
(billions of U.S. dollars)

***Redirecting Japan's growing trade surpluses can help meet Asia's growing external resource requirements.***

| | | | | *Projections* | |
|---|---|---|---|---|---|
| *Category* | *1989* | *1990* | *1991* | *1992* | *1993* |
| *High-income countries* | –43.9 | –69.8 | –10.8 | –12.7 | –10.3 |
| Japan | 57.0 | 35.8 | 72.6 | 92.6 | 93.4 |
| *Low- and middle-income countries* | –37.3 | –28.7 | –71.0 | –75.2 | –68.6 |
| East Asia | –5.9 | –5.6 | –15.6 | –20.4 | –26.0 |
| Europe and the FSU | –1.7 | –15.3 | –23.4 | –23.0 | –19.9 |
| Latin America and the Caribbean | 1.1 | 7.0 | –19.3 | –21.5 | –21.3 |

*Note:* In this table, East Asia comprises China, Fiji, Indonesia, Korea, Malaysia, Papua New Guinea, the Philippines, and Thailand.
*Source:* World Bank staff estimates.

in transition and for many environment-related investments, the need for—and the case for—concessional assistance will be strong in East Asia.

Most of these incremental resources could be generated from surplus economies in the region, particularly Japan and Taiwan (China). The issue of Japan's current account surplus is particularly important here. These surpluses are projected to remain above $90 billion during 1992–93. There are new pressures on Japan to increase its domestic consumption rate to reduce its surpluses. An alternative method will be restructuring these surpluses away from the OECD countries to the growing economies of East Asia. Such a restructuring will be feasible if concerted efforts are made to channel additional funds from Japan to East Asia for productive investment (including foreign direct investment).

The case for restructuring Japan's trade surpluses rests on recent trends in the direction of Japanese exports. Japan's exports to the United States stagnated at around $90 billion over 1988–91, whereas those to Asia increased by about 37 percent to reach $106 billion in 1991 (table 4.3). About 60 percent of the increase in Japanese exports in 1991 flowed to Asia. During the 1990s, Japan might have to rely increasingly on Asia for its markets—and that process can be facilitated by increased capital flows from Japan to Asia (particularly investment flows).

TABLE 4.3 CHANGING PATTERN OF JAPANESE EXPORTS
(billions of U.S. dollars)

***Developing Asia is now the largest and the most rapidly growing market for Japan.***

| *Value of exports* | *1988* | *1989* | *1990* | *1991* |
|---|---|---|---|---|
| Total | 264.9 | 274.6 | 287.7 | 314.9 |
| United States | 90.2 | 93.9 | 91.1 | 92.2 |
| Asia[a] | 77.4 | 82.6 | 90.1 | 105.9 |
| EC | 47.2 | 48.0 | 54.0 | 59.6 |

a. Including both South and East Asia, as defined in IMF, *Direction of Trade Statistics Yearbook,* which is the source of data for the table.

The region will have to address both domestic and external challenges in the years ahead. In the past, the external ups and downs were generally handled with enhanced export drives. As a result, the region's economies are even more fully integrated with the world economy than before, and that is a source of strength. But that also means increased vulnerability to external shocks in trade and financial flows. At this point, it is crucial to build on the strengths—keeping trade and capital flows open and fostering markets and the private sector. With the determination of its policymakers and the openness of its regional and global partners in development, there is every reason to believe that the 1990s will be another decade of solid performance for East Asia.

# Notes

1. The World Bank's East Asia and Pacific region comprises China, Fiji, Indonesia, Kiribati, Republic of Korea, Lao P.D.R., Malaysia, Maldives, Mongolia, Myanmar, Papua New Guinea, the Philippines, Solomon Islands, Thailand, Tonga, Vanuatu, Viet Nam, and Western Samoa. Throughout this report, the terms "East Asia" and "East Asia and the Pacific" are used interchangeably to refer to the East Asia and Pacific region.

2. All dollar amounts are U.S. dollars.

3. A billion is 1,000 million.

4. The problems remain serious in providing internationally comparable estimates of per capita incomes for China and other socialist economies in transition. To correct this problem, work is progressing on both the estimation of the local currency gross national product (GNP) and the conversion into a common currency.

5. Data refer to the income-weighted average of GDP growth per capita in China, Fiji, Indonesia, Korea, Malaysia, Papua New Guinea, the Philippines, and Thailand.

6. There are, of course, other possible groupings. For example, a paper by the Organization for Economic Cooperation and Development (OECD) classifies Korea, Taiwan (China), Hong Kong, and Singapore as the "first-tier" Asian newly industrialized economies (NIEs) and Malaysia, Thailand, Indonesia, and the Philippines as the "second-tier" Asian NIEs.

7. However, even when such monopolies arise, competitive alternatives can develop with technological change—for example, in long-distance telephone communications.

8. These cities are Shenyang, Xian, Beijing, Jakarta, Shanghai, Guangzhou, Iligan City, Bangkok, and Kuala Lumpur.

9. These cities are Shenyang, Seoul, Xian, Beijing, Manila, and Guangzhou.

# Bibliography


Asian Development Bank. 1992. *Asian Development Outlook 1992*. Manila.

Bhattacharya, Amar, and Johannes Linn. 1988. *Trade and Industrial Policies in the Developing Countries of East Asia*. World Bank Discussion Paper 27. Washington, D.C.

Cho, Yoon-Je, and Deena Khatkhate. 1989. *Lessons of Financial Liberalization in Asia: A Comparative Study*. World Bank Discussion Paper 50. Washington, D.C.

Easterly, William, Michael Kramer, Lant Pritchett, and Lawrence Summers. 1993. "Good Policy or Good Luck? Country Growth Performance and Temporary Shocks." Paper presented at conference, "How Do National Policies Affect Long-Run Growth," February. World Bank, Policy Research Department, Washington, D.C.

ESCAP. 1992. *State of the Environment in Asia and the Pacific*. Bangkok.

International Monetary Fund. 1992. *World Economic Outlook 1992*. Washington, D.C.

Johansen, Frida. 1992. "Poverty in East Asia." Mimeo. Office of the Vice President, East Asia and Pacific Region, World Bank, Washington, D.C.

Khatkhate, Deena R. 1992. *The Regulatory Impediments to the Private Industrial Sector Development in Asia*. World Bank Discussion Paper 177. Washington, D.C.

Leeds, Roger. 1988. "Malaysia: Genesis of a Privatization Transaction." Harvard University, Cambridge, Mass.

———. 1989. "Rebalancing the Public and Private Sectors: The Case of Malaysia." Organization for Economic Cooperation and Development, Paris.

Manasan, Rosario. 1990. "Management of Public Enterprises: The Case of the Philippines." Philippine Institute for Development Studies, Manila.

Nehru, Vikram. 1992. "East Asia and the Global Economy." Mimeo. World Bank, International Economics Department, Washington, D.C.

Song, Dae Hee. 1991a. "Reform of Korean Public Enterprise Sector and Privatization."

Korea Development Institute, Seoul.

———. 1991b. "Three Essays on Korean Privatization Policy." Korea Development Institute, Seoul.

Thomas, Vinod, and Yan Wang. 1992. "Government Policies and Productivity Growth: Is East Asia an Exception?" Mimeo. World Bank, East Asia and the Pacific Regional Office, Washington, D.C.

UN Center for Transnational Corporations (UNCTC). 1991. *Asia and the Pacific,* Volume I of *World Investment Directory 1991*. New York: United Nations.

World Bank. 1990. *Indonesia: A Strategy for Sustained Reduction in Poverty*. Washington, D.C.

———. 1991. *World Development Report 1991*. New York: Oxford University Press.

———. 1992a. *China: Reform and the Role of the Plan in the 1990s*. Washington, D.C.

———. 1992b. *China: Strategies for Reducing Poverty in the 1990s*. Washington, D.C.

———. 1992c. *Global Economic Prospects and the Developing Countries*. Washington, D.C.

———. 1992d. *Social Indicators of Development, 1991–92*. Washington, D.C.

———. 1992e. *World Development Report 1992*. New York: Oxford University Press.

———. 1992f. *The World Bank Atlas, 25th Anniversary Edition*. Washington, D.C.

World Economic Forum. 1992. *World Competitiveness Report 1992*. Geneva.

World Resources Institute. 1992. *World Resources 1992–93: Toward Sustainable Development*. New York: Oxford University Press.

# Regional Development Indicators

The letter w means weighted average; m, median value; t, total.

The symbol .. means not available.

The figures 0 and 0.0 mean zero or less than half the unit shown.

A blank means not applicable.

Figures with asterisks indicate data that are for years or periods other than those specified.

Except as noted, the data are derived from the World Bank's central data base.

The classification of economies by region and income is presented in table 29.

Note that cross-country comparisons of these data have limitations, especially in the case of social indicators. (See World Bank 1992e, p. 210, for a discussion.)

## Table A. Selected Economic Indicators, 1991

| Country | GNP per capita (U.S. dollars) | Growth rates (percent) | | | | Inflation rate (percent) | Percentage of GDP | | | |
|---|---|---|---|---|---|---|---|---|---|---|
| | | GDP | Manufacturing | Exports GNFS | Imports GNFS | | Gross domestic investment | Gross domestic saving | Resource balance | Current account balance |
| China | 370 | 6.4 | 11.4 | 14.4 | 17.9 | 4.5 | 35.8 | 38.8 | 3.0 | 3.6 |
| Fiji | 1830 | -0.1 | 4.2 | .. | .. | 6.5 | 16.2 | 17.2 | 1.2 | -2.5 |
| Indonesia | 610 | 6.6 | 9.8 | 24.3 | 13.6 | 9.2 | 35.1 | 35.7 | 1.0 | -3.6 |
| Korea | 6350 | 8.4 | 8.5 | 9.8 | 17.4 | 9.7 | 39.1 | 36.5 | -2.9 | -3.0 |
| Lao P.D.R. | 220 | 4.0 | 34.3 | -0.8 | 8.4 | 13.6 | .. | .. | -10.8 | -11.4 |
| Malaysia | 2500 | 8.8 | 14.0 | 13.3 | 19.8 | 4.4 | 35.9 | 30.4 | -5.2 | -9.3 |
| Mongolia | .. | -16.2 | .. | .. | .. | 120.0 | .. | .. | .. | .. |
| Papua New Guinea | 820 | 9.5 | 15.8 | 15.8 | 20.1 | 7.0 | 27.4 | 17.5 | -7.2 | -15.4 |
| Philippines | 740 | -1.0 | -0.9 | 4.6 | -3.1 | 18.7 | 20.0 | 18.9 | -3.3 | -2.4 |
| Solomon Islands | 690 | 3.0 | 3.4 | .. | .. | 15.1 | 28.0 | -1.6 | -27.5 | -33.5 |
| Thailand | 1580 | 8.0 | 9.5 | 11.0 | 10.9 | 5.7 | 38.9 | 31.7 | -7.5 | -8.5 |

GNFS: goods and nonfactor services.
*Source*: World Bank staff estimates

# Table 1. Basic Indicators

| Country or group | Population (millions) mid-1990 | Area (thousands of square kilometers) | GNP per capita[a] Dollars 1990 | GNP per capita[a] Average annual growth rate (percent) 1965–90 | Average annual rate of inflation (percent)[a] 1965–80 | Average annual rate of inflation (percent)[a] 1980–90 | Life expectancy at birth (years) 1990 | Adult illiteracy (percent) Female 1990 | Adult illiteracy (percent) Total 1990 |
|---|---|---|---|---|---|---|---|---|---|
| **GROUP AVERAGES** | | | | | | | | | |
| Low-income economies | 3058.3 t | 37780 t | 350 t | 2.9 w | 8 w | 9.6 w | 62 w | 52 w | 40 w |
| Middle-income economies | 1087.5 t | 41139 t | 2320 t | 2.2 w | 21.1 w | 85.6 w | 66 w | 27 w | 22 w |
| Low- and middle-income econ. | 4145.8 t | 78919 t | 870 t | 2.5 w | 16.7 w | 61.8 w | 63 w | 46 w | 36 w |
| Sub-Saharan Africa | 495.2 t | 23066 t | 340 t | 0.2 w | 11.4 w | 20 w | 51 w | 62 w | 50 w |
| **East Asia & Pacific** | **1577.2 t** | **15572 t** | **600 t** | **5.3 w** | **9.3 w** | **6 w** | **68 w** | **34 w** | **24 w** |
| South Asia | 1147.7 t | 5158 t | 340 t | 1.9 w | 8.3 w | 8 w | 58 w | 67 w | 53 w |
| Europe | 200.3 t | 2171 t | .. t | .. w | 13.9 w | 38.8 w | 70 w | 22 w | 15 w |
| Middle East & N. Africa | 256.4 t | 11334 t | .. t | 1.8 w | 13.6 w | 7.5 w | 61 w | 60 w | 47 w |
| Latin America & Caribbean | 433.1 t | 20397 t | 2180 t | 1.7 w | 31.4 w | 192.1 w | 68 w | 18 w | 16 w |
| **EAST ASIA AND PACIFIC** | | | | | | | | | |
| ***Asian tigers*** | | | | | | | | | |
| Korea, Rep. | 42.8 | 99 | 5400 | 7.1 | 18.4 | 5.1 | 70 | 7 | 4 |
| Malaysia | 17.9 | 330 | 2320 | 4 | 4.9 | 1.6 | 70 | 30 | 22 |
| Thailand | 55.8 | 513 | 1420 | 4.4 | 6.2 | 3.4 | 66 | 10 | 7 |
| ***Socialist economies in transition*** | | | | | | | | | |
| Cambodia | 8.5 | 181 | .. | .. | .. | .. | 50 | 78 | 65 |
| China | 1133.7 | 9561 | 370 | 5.8 | -0.3 | 5.8 | 70 | 38 | 27 |
| Lao P.D.R. | 4.1 | 237 | 200 | .. | .. | .. | 49 | .. | .. |
| Mongolia | 2.1 | 1567 | .. | .. | .. | -1.3 | 63 | .. | .. |
| Myanmar | 41.6 | 677 | .. | 1.7 | 8.6 | 11.4 | 61 | 28 | 19 |
| Viet Nam | 66.3 | 332 | .. | .. | .. | .. | 67 | 16 | 12 |
| ***Large island economies*** | | | | | | | | | |
| Indonesia | 178.2 | 1905 | 570 | 4.5 | 35.5 | 8.4 | 62 | 32 | 23 |
| Papua New Guinea | 3.9 | 463 | 860 | 0.1 | 8.1 | 5.3 | 55 | 62 | 48 |
| Philippines | 61.5 | 300 | 730 | 1.3 | 11.4 | 14.9 | 64 | 11 | 10 |

| | | | | | | | | | |
|---|---|---|---|---|---|---|---|---|---|
| ***Pacific island economies*** | | | | | | | | | |
| Fiji | 0.7 | 18 | 1780 | 1.9 | 10.3 | 5.4 | 65 | .. | .. |
| Kiribati | 0.1 | 1 | 760 | .. | .. | 5.5 | 55 | .. | .. |
| Maldives | 0.2 | 0 | 450 | 2.8 | .. | .. | 62 | .. | .. |
| Solomon Islands | 0.3 | 29 | 590 | .. | 7.7 | 10 | 65 | .. | .. |
| Tonga | 0.1 | 1 | 1010 | .. | .. | .. | 67 | .. | .. |
| Vanuatu | 0.2 | 12 | 1100 | .. | .. | 4.9 | 65 | .. | .. |
| Western Samoa | 0.2 | 3 | 730 | .. | .. | 9.2 | 66 | .. | .. |
| ***Other*** | | | | | | | | | |
| Hong Kong | 5.8 | 1 | 11490[b] | 6.2 | 8.1 | 7.2 | 78 | .. | .. |
| Japan | 123.5 | 378 | 25430 | 4.1 | 7.7 | 1.5 | 79 | .. | .. |
| Singapore | 3 | 1 | 11160 | 6.5 | 5.1 | 1.7 | 74 | .. | .. |
| **MEMORANDUM ITEMS** | | | | | | | | | |
| United States | 250 | 9373 | 21790 | 1.7 | 6.5 | 3.7 | 76 | .. | .. |
| European Community | 344.3 t | 2334 t | 16030 t | 2.4 w | 8.8 w | 6 w | 76 w | 7 w | 5 w |
| India | 849.5 | 3288 | 350 | 1.9 | 7.5 | 7.9 | 59 | 66 | 52 |
| Bangladesh | 106.7 | 144 | 210 | 0.7 | 15.9 | 9.6 | 52 | 78 | 65 |
| Nigeria | 115.5 | 924 | 290 | 0.1 | 14.6 | 17.7 | 52 | 61 | 49 |
| Tanzania | 24.5 | 945 | .. | -0.2 | 9.6 | 25.8 | 48 | .. | .. |
| Turkey | 56.1 | 779 | 1630 | 2.6 | 20.8 | 43.2 | 67 | 29 | 19 |
| Hungary | 10.6 | 93 | 2780 | .. | 2.6 | 9 | 71 | .. | .. |
| Poland | 38.2 | 313 | 1690 | .. | .. | 54.3 | 71 | .. | .. |
| Egypt, Arab Rep. | 52.1 | 1001 | 600 | 4.1 | 6.4 | 11.8 | 60 | 66 | 52 |
| Argentina | 32.3 | 2767 | 2370 | -0.3 | 78.4 | 394.7 | 71 | 5 | 5 |
| Brazil | 150.4 | 8512 | 2680 | 3.3 | 31.3 | 284.3 | 66 | 20 | 19 |
| Chile | 13.2 | 757 | 1940 | 0.4 | 129.9 | 20.5 | 72 | 7 | 7 |
| Mexico | 86.2 | 1958 | 2490 | 2.8 | 13 | 70.3 | 70 | 15 | 13 |

a. Methodology used in World Bank 1992f.
b. GDP per capita.

# Table 2. Growth of Production

| Country or group | Average annual growth rate (percent) | | | | | | | | | |
|---|---|---|---|---|---|---|---|---|---|---|
| | GDP | | Agriculture | | Industry | | Manufacturing[a] | | Services, etc.[b] | |
| | *1965–80* | *1980–90* | *1965–80* | *1980–90* | *1965–80* | *1980–90* | *1965–80* | *1980–90* | *1965–80* | *1980–90* |
| **GROUP AVERAGES** | | | | | | | | | | |
| Low-income economies | 4.9 w | 6.1 w | 2.6 w | 3.9 w | 7.3 w | 8.2 w | 6.7 w | 11.1 w | 6.2 w | 6.5 w |
| Middle-income economies | 6.3 w | 2.5 w | 3.4 w | 2.4 w | 6.7 w | 2.3 w | .. w | 3.5 w | 7.1 w | 2.7 w |
| Low-and middle-income econ. | 5.9 w | 3.6 w | 2.9 w | 3.2 w | 6.8 w | 3.8 w | 8 w | 6 w | 6.9 w | 3.6 w |
| Sub-Saharan Africa | 4.2 w | 2.1 w | 2 w | 2.1 w | 7.2 w | 2 w | .. w | 3.1 w | 4.6 w | 2.5 w |
| **East Asia & Pacific** | **7.3 w** | **7.8 w** | **3.2 w** | **4.8 w** | **10.8 w** | **10.2 w** | **10.3 w** | **12.4 w** | **8.9 w** | **8 w** |
| South Asia | 3.6 w | 5.2 w | 2.5 w | 3 w | 4.3 w | 6.5 w | 4.5 w | 6.8 w | 4.5 w | 6.3 w |
| Europe | .. w | 2.1 w | .. w | 1 w | .. w | 2.7 w | .. w | .. w | .. w | 2.7 w |
| Middle East & North Africa | 6.7 w | 2 w | 4.3 w | 4.3 w | 6.3 w | 0.7 w | .. w | 3.4 w | 8.7 w | 2.2 w |
| Latin America & Caribbean | 6 w | 1.6 w | 3.1 w | 2 w | 6.6 w | 1.2 w | 8.3 w | 1.7 w | 6.6 w | 1.7 w |
| **EAST ASIA AND PACIFIC** | | | | | | | | | | |
| ***Asian tigers*** | | | | | | | | | | |
| Korea, Rep. | 9.9 | 9.7 | 3 | 2.8 | 16.4 | 12.2 | 18.7 | 12.7 | 9.6 | 9.2 |
| Malaysia | 7.4 | 5.2 | .. | .. | .. | .. | .. | .. | .. | .. |
| Thailand | 7.3 | 7.6 | 4.6 | 4.1 | 9.5 | 9 | 11.2 | 8.9 | 7.4 | 7.8 |
| ***Socialist economies in transition*** | | | | | | | | | | |
| Cambodia | .. | .. | .. | .. | .. | .. | .. | .. | .. | .. |
| China | 6.8 | 9.5 | 2.8 | 6.1 | 10 | 12.5 | 8.9 * | 14.4 * | 11.9 | 9.1 |
| Lao P.D.R. | .. | .. | .. | .. | .. | .. | .. | .. | .. | .. |
| Mongolia | .. | 5.6 * | .. | .. | .. | .. | .. | .. | .. | .. |
| Myanmar | 4 | 0.7 | 3.7 | 0.7 | 4.2 | 0.6 | 3.9 | -0.2 | 4.2 | 0.8 |
| Viet Nam | .. | .. | .. | .. | .. | .. | .. | .. | .. | .. |
| ***Large island economies*** | | | | | | | | | | |
| Indonesia | 7 | 5.5 | 4.3 | 3.2 | 11.9 | 5.6 | 12 | 12.5 | 7.3 | 6.7 |
| Papua New Guinea | 4.1 | 1.9 | 3.1 | 1.7 | .. | 2.7 | .. | 1.9 | .. | 1.4 |
| Philippines | 5.7 | 0.9 | 3.9 | 1 | 7.7 | -0.8 | 6.8 | 0.1 | 5 | 2.6 |

| | | | | | | | | | | |
|---|---|---|---|---|---|---|---|---|---|---|
| ***Pacific island economies*** | | | | | | | | | | |
| Fiji | 6 | 1.6 | 2.4 | 1.7 | 4.2 | -1.1 | 3.7 | 1.1 | 9.2 | 2.6 |
| Kiribati | .. | .. | .. | .. | .. | .. | .. | .. | .. | .. |
| Maldives | .. | .. | .. | .. | .. | .. | .. | .. | .. | .. |
| Solomon Islands | .. | .. | .. | .. | .. | .. | .. | .. | .. | .. |
| Tonga | .. | .. | .. | .. | .. | .. | .. | .. | .. | .. |
| Vanuatu | .. | 3.1 | .. | 2.1 * | .. | .. | .. | .. | .. | .. |
| Western Samoa | .. | .. | .. | .. | .. | .. | .. | .. | .. | .. |
| ***Other*** | | | | | | | | | | |
| Hong Kong | 8.6 | 7.1 * | .. | .. | .. | .. | .. | .. | .. | .. |
| Japan | 6.4 | 4.1 * | -0.6 | 1.3 * | 7.1 | 4.5 * | 7.8 | 5.3 * | 6.8 | 3.8 * |
| Singapore | 10 | 6.4 | 2.8 | -6.2 | 11.9 | 5.4 | 13.2 | 6.6 | 9.1 | 7.2 |
| **MEMORANDUM ITEMS** | | | | | | | | | | |
| United States | 2.7 | 3.4 * | 1 | .. | 1.7 | .. | 2.6 | .. | 3.3 | .. |
| European Community | 3.6 w | 2.4 w | .. w | 1.1 w | .. w | 0.9 w | .. w | 1.8 w | .. w | 2.7 w |
| India | 3.6 | 5.3 | 2.5 | 3.1 | 4.2 | 6.6 | 4.5 | 7.1 | 4.4 | 6.5 |
| Bangladesh | 1.7 | 4.3 | 0.6 | 2.6 | 1.5 | 4.9 | 2.8 | 2.8 | 3.6 | 5.8 |
| Nigeria | 6 | 1.4 | 1.7 | 3.3 | 13.1 | -1.2 | 14.6 | -1 | 5.9 | 2.7 |
| Tanzania | 3.9 | 2.8 | 1.6 | 4.1 | 4.2 | 0 | 5.6 | -0.4 | 10.8 | 1.3 |
| Turkey | 6.2 | 5.1 | 3.2 | 3 | 7.2 | 6.2 | 7.5 | 7.2 | 7.6 | 5.2 |
| Hungary | 5.7 | 1.3 | 2.7 | 1.6 | 6.4 | -0.5 | .. | .. | 6.2 | 2.8 |
| Poland | .. | 1.8 | .. | .. | .. | .. | .. | .. | .. | .. |
| Egypt, Arab Rep. | 7.3 | 5 | 2.7 | 2.5 | 6.9 | 4.3 | .. | .. | 13.7 | 6.7 |
| Argentina | 3.4 | -0.5 | 1.4 | 1.2 | 3.3 | -1.4 | .. | .. | 4.1 | 0 |
| Brazil | 9 | 2.7 | 3.8 | 2.8 | 10.1 | 2.1 | 9.8 | 1.7 | 9.4 | 3.4 |
| Chile | 1.9 | 3.2 | .. | .. | .. | .. | .. | .. | .. | .. |
| Mexico | 6.5 | 1 | 3.2 | 0.4 | 7.6 | 1 | 7.4 | 1.4 | 6.5 | 1.1 |

a. Because manufacturing is generally the most dynamic part of the industrial sector, its share of GDP is shown separately.

b. Services, etc. includes unallocated items.

# Table 3. Structure of Production

| Country or group | GDP[a] (millions of dollars) 1965 | GDP[a] (millions of dollars) 1990 | Agriculture 1965 | Agriculture 1990 | Industry 1965 | Industry 1990 | Manufacturing[a] 1965 | Manufacturing[a] 1990 | Services, etc.[b] 1965 | Services, etc.[b] 1990 |
|---|---|---|---|---|---|---|---|---|---|---|
| | *Distribution of gross domestic product (percent)* | | | | | | | | | |
| **GROUP AVERAGES** | | | | | | | | | | |
| Low-income economies | 168825 w | 915585 w | 41 w | 31 w | 26 w | 36 w | 19 w | 27 w | 32 w | 39 |
| Middle-income economies | 209744 w | 2451319 w | 19 w | 12 w | 34 w | 37 w | 20 w | .. w | 46 w | 51 |
| Low-and middle-income econ. | 384126 w | 3347401 w | 29 w | 17 w | 31 w | 37 w | 20 w | 25 w | 40 w | 47 |
| Sub-Saharan Africa | 27039 w | 163015 w | 41 w | 32 w | 20 w | 30 w | 7 w | .. w | 39 w | 40 |
| **East Asia & Pacific** | **92624 w** | **821246 w** | **37 w** | **21 w** | **32 w** | **45 w** | **24 w** | **34 w** | **30 w** | **43** |
| South Asia | 64509 w | 345639 w | 44 w | 33 w | 21 w | 26 w | 15 w | 17 w | 35 w | 41 |
| Europe | .. w | 489254 w | .. w | 12 w | .. w | 31 w | .. w | .. w | .. w | 43 |
| Middle East & N.Africa | 27956 w | .. w | 20 w | .. w | 36 w | .. w | 10 w | .. w | 40 w | .. |
| Latin America & Caribbean | 102604 w | 1020190 w | 16 w | 10 w | 34 w | 36 w | 23 w | 25 w | 51 w | 54 |
| **EAST ASIA AND PACIFIC** | | | | | | | | | | |
| ***Asian tigers*** | | | | | | | | | | |
| Korea, Rep. | 2996 | 236397 | 38 | 9 | 25 | 45 | 18 | 31 | 37 | 46 |
| Malaysia | 3130 | 42398 | 28 | .. | 25 | .. | 9 | .. | 47 | .. |
| Thailand | 4389 | 80172 | 32 | 12 | 23 | 39 | 14 | 26 | 45 | 48 |
| ***Socialist economies in transition*** | | | | | | | | | | |
| Cambodia | 869 | .. | .. | .. | .. | .. | .. | .. | .. | .. |
| China | 67199 | 364903 | 38 | 27 | 35 | 42 | 28 | 38 | 27 | 31 |
| Lao P.D.R. | .. | 865 | .. | .. | .. | .. | .. | .. | .. | .. |
| Mongolia | .. | 2251 | .. | 17 | .. | 34 | .. | .. | .. | 49 |
| Myanmar | 1601 | 22197 | 35 | 57 | 13 | 11 | 9 | 8 | 52 | 32 |
| Viet Nam | .. | 9072 | .. | .. | .. | .. | .. | .. | .. | .. |
| ***Large island economies*** | | | | | | | | | | |
| Indonesia | 5981 * | 107293 | 51 * | 22 | 13 * | 40 | 8 * | 20 | 36 * | 38 |
| Papua New Guinea | 344 | 3288 | 42 | 29 | 18 | 31 | .. | 12 | 41 | 40 |
| Philippines | 6010 | 43861 | 26 | 22 | 27 | 35 | 20 | 25 | 47 | 43 |

| | | | | | | | | | | |
|---|---|---|---|---|---|---|---|---|---|---|
| ***Pacific island economies*** | | | | | | | | | | |
| Fiji | 132 | 1228 | 34 | 20 | 25 | 20 | 17 | 10 | 41 | 59 |
| Kiribati | .. | 30 | .. | 30 | .. | 8 | .. | 2 | .. | 62 |
| Maldives | .. | 101 | .. | .. | .. | .. | .. | .. | .. | .. |
| Solomon Islands | .. | 155 * | .. | .. | .. | .. | .. | .. | .. | .. |
| Tonga | .. | .. | .. | .. | .. | .. | .. | .. | .. | .. |
| Vanuatu | .. | 141 * | .. | 19 * | .. | 13 * | .. | 5 * | .. | 68 |
| Western Samoa | .. | .. | .. | .. | .. | .. | .. | .. | .. | .. |
| ***Other*** | | | | | | | | | | |
| Hong Kong | 2151 | 59668 * | 2 | 0 * | 40 | 26 * | 24 | 18 * | 58 | 73 |
| Japan | 91294 | 2942890 | 10 | 3 * | 44 | 42 * | 34 | 28 * | 46 | 56 |
| Singapore | 966 | 34599 | 3 | 0 | 24 | 37 | 15 | 29 | 74 | 63 |
| **MEMORANDUM ITEMS** | | | | | | | | | | |
| United States | 701380 | 5392199 | 3 | .. | 38 | .. | 28 | .. | 59 | .. |
| European Community | 464730 w | 6004564 w | .. w | .. w | .. w | .. w | .. w | .. w | .. w | .. |
| India | 50531 | 254543 | 44 | 31 | 22 | 29 | 16 | 19 | 34 | 40 |
| Bangladesh | 4377 | 22884 | 53 | 38 | 11 | 15 | 5 | 9 | 36 | 46 |
| Nigeria | 5375 | 34756 | 55 | 36 | 12 | 38 | 5 | 7 * | 33 | 25 |
| Tanzania | 794 | 2059 | 46 | 59 * | 14 | 12 * | 8 | 10 * | 40 | 29 |
| Turkey | 7656 | 96500 | 34 | 18 | 25 | 33 | 16 | 24 | 41 | 49 |
| Hungary | .. | 32923 | .. | 12 | .. | 32 | .. | 27 | .. | 56 |
| Poland | .. | 63590 | .. | 14 | .. | 36 | .. | .. | .. | 50 |
| Egypt, Arab Rep. | 4547 | 33205 | 29 | 17 | 27 | 29 | .. | 16 | 45 | 53 |
| Argentina | 19412 | 93476 | 17 | 15 | 42 | 40 | 33 | .. | 42 | 46 |
| Brazil | 19467 | 414061 | 19 | 10 | 33 | 39 | 26 | 26 | 48 | 51 |
| Chile | 5879 | 27791 | 9 | .. | 40 | .. | 24 | .. | 52 | .. |
| Mexico | 21636 | 237748 | 14 | 9 | 27 | 30 | 20 | 23 | 59 | 61 |

a. Because manufacturing is generally the most dynamic part of the industrial sector, its share of GDP is shown separately.

b. Services, etc. includes unallocated items.

# Table 4. Agriculture and Food

| Country or group | Value added in agriculture (millions of current dollars) 1970 | 1990 | Cereal imports (thousands of metric tons) 1974 | 1990 | Food aid in cereals (thousands of metric tons) 1974/75 | 1989/90 | Fertilizer consumption (hundreds of grams of plant nutrient per hectare of arable land) 1970/71 | 1989/90 | Average index of food production per capita (1979–81=100) 1988–90 |
|---|---|---|---|---|---|---|---|---|---|
| **GROUP AVERAGES** | | | | | | | | | |
| Low-income economies | 84469 w | 287958 w | 26538 t | 35748 t | 6643 t | 6599 t | 178 t | 946 t | 119 w |
| Middle-income economies | 48705 w | 285203 w | 39280 t | 77607 t | 1284 t | 4483 t | 363 t | 693 t | 102 w |
| Low-and middle-income econ. | 136424 w | 581154 w | 65818 t | 113355 t | 7928 t | 11083 t | 256 t | 833 t | 115 w |
| Sub-Saharan Africa | 13167 w | 51410 w | 4209 t | 7838 t | 910 t | 2677 t | 33 t | 89 t | 94 w |
| **East Asia & Pacific** | **44838 w** | **176368 w** | **14946 t** | **30955 t** | **923 t** | **391 t** | **364 t** | **1903 t** | **127 w** |
| South Asia | 32980 w | 112436 w | 9404 t | 5274 t | 4522 t | 2264 t | 135 t | 689 t | 116 w |
| Europe | .. w | 59446 w | 13564 t | 11030 t | 16 t | 1595 t | 878 t | 1424 t | 102 w |
| Middle East & N. Africa | 7248 w | 58699 w | 11879 t | 38083 t | 993 t | 2373 t | 138 t | 646 t | 101 w |
| Latin America & Caribbean | 19631 w | 103594 w | 11690 t | 19299 t | 563 t | 1783 t | 177 t | 439 t | 106 w |
| **EAST ASIA AND PACIFIC** | | | | | | | | | |
| ***Asian tigers*** | | | | | | | | | |
| Korea, Rep. | 2311 | 21364 | 2679 | 9087 | 234 | .. | 2450 | 4250 | 106 |
| Malaysia | 1198 | .. | 1023 | 2582 | 1 | 1 | 436 | 1572 | 147 |
| Thailand | 1837 | 9948 | 97 | 387 | .. | 95 | 59 | 365 | 106 |
| ***Socialist economies in transition*** | | | | | | | | | |
| Cambodia | .. | .. | 223 | 20 | 226 | 11 | 11 | .. | 165 |
| China | 31821 | 100348 | 6033 | 13719 | .. | 84 | 410 | 2619 | 133 |
| Lao P.D.R. | .. | .. | 53 | 54 | 8 | 29 | 2 | 3 | 114 |
| Mongolia | .. | 390 | 28 | 57 | .. | .. | 22 | 124 | 86 |
| Myanmar | 819 | 12667 | 26 | .. | 9 | .. | 21 | 86 | 93 |
| Viet Nam | .. | .. | 1854 | 204 | 64 | 72 | 513 | 841 | 127 |
| ***Large island economies*** | | | | | | | | | |
| Indonesia | 4340 | 23368 | 1919 | 1828 | 301 | 39 | 133 | 1166 | 123 |
| Papua New Guinea | 240 | 942 | 71 | 222 | .. | 0 | 58 | 399 | 103 |
| Philippines | 1975 | 9686 | 817 | 2545 | 89 | 59 | 287 | 674 | 84 |

| | | | | | | | | | |
|---|---|---|---|---|---|---|---|---|---|
| ***Pacific island economies*** | | | | | | | | | |
| Fiji | 55 | 248 | 62 | 94 | .. | .. | 264 | 960 | 86 |
| Kiribati | .. | .. | 4 | 8 | .. | .. | .. | .. | .. |
| Maldives | .. | .. | 6 | 26 | .. | 3 | .. | .. | 97 |
| Solomon Islands | .. | .. | 5 | 13 | .. | .. | .. | .. | 82 |
| Tonga | .. | .. | 6 | 7 | .. | .. | .. | .. | 78 |
| Vanuatu | .. | 27 * | 6 | 7 | .. | .. | .. | .. | 87 |
| Western Samoa | .. | .. | 6 | 11 | .. | 1 | .. | .. | 96 |
| ***Other*** | | | | | | | | | |
| Hong Kong | 62 | 181 * | 657 | 754 | .. | .. | .. | .. | 80 |
| Japan | 12467 | 74085 * | 19557 | 27008 | .. | .. | 3547 | 4179 | 101 |
| Singapore | 44 | 97 | 682 | 737 | 0 | .. | 2500 | 5600 | 69 |
| **MEMORANDUM ITEMS** | | | | | | | | | |
| United States | 27856 | .. | 460 | 2217 | .. | .. | 816 | 985 | 92 |
| European Community | 26841 w | .. w | 47042 t | 33430 t | .. t | .. t | 1880 t | 2419 t | 107 w |
| India | 23916 | 78099 | 5261 | 447 | 1582 | 456 | 137 | 687 | 119 |
| Bangladesh | 3650 | 8721 | 1866 | 1726 | 2076 | 1134 | 157 | 993 | 96 |
| Nigeria | 4787 | 12582 | 389 | 502 | 7 | .. | 2 | 121 | 106 |
| Tanzania | 483 | 1444 * | 431 | 73 | 148 | 22 | 31 | 93 | 88 |
| Turkey | 3383 | 17485 | 1276 | 3177 | 16 | 13 | 157 | 645 | 97 |
| Hungary | 1010 | 4091 | 408 | 503 | .. | .. | 1497 | 2463 | 113 |
| Poland | .. | 8775 | 4185 | 1550 | .. | 1582 | 1678 | 2052 | 109 |
| Egypt, Arab Rep. | 1942 | 5771 | 3877 | 8580 | 610 | 1210 | 1312 | 4043 | 118 |
| Argentina | 2693 | 12405 | 0 | 4 | .. | .. | 26 | 46 | 93 |
| Brazil | 4388 | 42288 | 2485 | 3421 | 31 | 20 | 186 | 430 | 115 |
| Chile | 557 | .. | 1737 | 247 | 323 | 4 | 322 | 800 | 113 |
| Mexico | 4462 | 21074 | 2881 | 7648 | .. | 341 | 232 | 728 | 102 |

# Table 5. Commercial Energy

| | Average annual energy growth rate (percent) | | | | Energy consumption per capita (kilograms of oil equivalent) | | Energy imports as a percentage of merchandise exports | |
|---|---|---|---|---|---|---|---|---|
| | Energy production | | Energy consumption | | | | | |
| *Country or group* | *1965–80* | *1980–90* | *1965–80* | *1980–90* | *1965* | *1990* | *1965* | *1990* |
| **GROUP AVERAGES** | | | | | | | | |
| Low-income economies | 10 w | 4.7 w | 8.2 w | 5.5 w | 124 w | 339 w | 7 w | 4 w |
| Middle-income economies | 5.1 w | 1.9 w | 6.1 w | 3.6 w | 712 w | 1357 w | 8 w | 14 w |
| Low-and middle-income econ. | 6.2 w | 2.8 w | 6.8 w | 4.3 w | 277 w | 605 w | 8 w | 10 w |
| Sub-Saharan Africa | 15.5 w | 2.8 w | 5.3 w | 2.6 w | 74 w | 103 w | 7 w | 28 w |
| **East Asia & Pacific** | **10 w** | **5.4 w** | **9.4 w** | **5.7 w** | **164 w** | **553 w** | **10 w** | **8 w** |
| South Asia | 5.8 w | 7 w | 5.7 w | 6 w | 90 w | 205 w | 7 w | .. |
| Europe | 3.3 w | 1.7 w | 5.2 w | 2 w | 1372 w | 2677 w | 12 w | 19 w |
| Middle East & North Africa | 7.1 w | 0.6 w | 8.4 w | 7.8 w | 355 w | 1102 w | 3 w | 20 w |
| Latin America & Caribbean | 1.9 w | 2.5 w | 6.2 w | 2.7 w | 579 w | 1057 w | 8 w | 5 w |
| **EAST ASIA AND PACIFIC** | | | | | | | | |
| ***Asian tigers*** | | | | | | | | |
| Korea, Rep. | 4.1 | 10.4 | 12.1 | 8.1 | 238 | 1898 | 18 | 12 |
| Malaysia | 36.9 | 14.4 | 6.7 | 7.8 | 313 | 974 | 11 | 4 * |
| Thailand | 9 | 26.2 | 10.1 | 7.2 | 82 | 352 | 11 | 10 * |
| ***Socialist economies in transition*** | | | | | | | | |
| Cambodia | .. | 4.9 | 7.6 | 2.5 | 19 | 59 | .. | .. |
| China | 10 | 5.5 | 9.8 | 5.6 | 178 | 598 | .. | 3 |
| Lao P.D.R. | .. | 0.5 | 4.2 | 1.8 | 24 | 39 | .. | .. |
| Mongolia | 10.3 | 3 | 9.6 | 3.1 | 461 | 1277 | .. | .. |
| Myanmar | 8.4 | 4.4 | 4.9 | 4.8 | 39 | 82 | 4 | 4 * |
| Viet Nam | 5.3 | 2.5 | -2.6 | 2.6 | 97 | 100 | .. | 1 * |
| ***Large island economies*** | | | | | | | | |
| Indonesia | 9.9 | 1 | 8.4 | 4.1 | 91 | 272 | 3 | 6 |
| Papua New Guinea | 13.7 | 5.9 | 13 | 2.4 | 56 | 233 | 7 | .. |
| Philippines | 9 | 7.5 | 5.8 | 2.3 | 158 | 215 | 12 | 17 * |

| | | | | | | | | |
|---|---|---|---|---|---|---|---|---|
| ***Pacific island economies*** | | | | | | | | |
| Fiji | .. | .. | 4.5 | 1.4 | 384 | 538 | 17 | 20 * |
| Kiribati | .. | .. | 4.2 | -2.3 | 89 | 114 | .. | .. |
| Maldives | .. | .. | .. | 9.1 | 0 | 144 | .. | .. |
| Solomon Islands | .. | .. | 16.7 | -22.8 | 305 | 180 | .. | 8 * |
| Tonga | .. | .. | 9 | 2.5 | 54 | 182 | .. | .. |
| Vanuatu | .. | .. | 5.8 | 1.6 | 197 | 298 | .. | .. |
| Western Samoa | .. | .. | .. | .. | .. | 423 | 6 | 95 * |
| ***Other*** | | | | | | | | |
| Hong Kong | .. | .. | 7.5 | 3.9 | 584 | 1717 | 6 | 6 |
| Japan | -0.4 | 4.2 | 6.1 | 2.1 | 1474 | 3563 | 19 | 16 |
| Singapore | .. | .. | 5.7 | 5.8 | 2214 | 5685 | 17 | 15 |
| **MEMORANDUM ITEMS** | | | | | | | | |
| United States | 1.1 | 0.8 | 2.3 | 1.5 | 6535 | 7822 | 8 | 16 |
| European Community | 2.8 w | 1.4 w | 3.1 w | 1 w | 2243 w | 3319 w | 13 w | 9 w |
| India | 5.6 | 7 | 5.8 | 5.9 | 100 | 231 | 8 | 24 * |
| Bangladesh | .. | 12.1 | .. | 7.9 | 0 | 57 | .. | 4 * |
| Nigeria | 17.3 | 0.2 | 12.9 | 4.8 | 34 | 138 | 7 | 4 * |
| Tanzania | 7.3 | 3.2 | 3.7 | 2 | 37 | 38 | .. | 4 * |
| Turkey | 4.3 | 8.5 | 8.5 | 6.9 | 257 | 857 | 12 | 28 |
| Hungary | 0.8 | 1.1 | 3.8 | 1.4 | 1825 | 3211 | 12 | 11 |
| Poland | 4 | 1.1 | 4.8 | 1.2 | 2027 | 3416 | .. | .. |
| Egypt, Arab Rep. | 10.7 | 4.8 | 6.2 | 5 | 313 | 598 | 11 | 10 * |
| Argentina | 4.5 | 3.3 | 4.3 | 3.5 | 975 | 1801 | 8 | 5 * |
| Brazil | 8.6 | 7.9 | 9.9 | 4.9 | 286 | 915 | 14 | 14 * |
| Chile | 1.8 | 3.1 | 3 | 2.9 | 652 | 887 | 5 | 9 * |
| Mexico | 9.7 | 1.3 | 7.9 | 1.2 | 605 | 1300 | 4 | 4 |

# Table 6. Structure of Manufacturing

| Country or group | Value added in manufacturing (millions of current dollars) | | Distribution of manufacturing value added (percent; current prices): Food, beverages, and tobacco | | Textiles and clothing | | Machinery and transport equipment | | Chemicals | |
|---|---|---|---|---|---|---|---|---|---|---|
| | 1970 | 1989 | 1970 | 1989 | 1970 | 1989 | 1970 | 1989 | 1970 | 1989 |
| **GROUP AVERAGES** | | | | | | | | | | |
| Low-income economies | 43830 w | 243089 w | | | | | | | | |
| Middle-income economies | 67652 w | 573015 w | | | | | | | | |
| Low-and middle-income econ. | 113627 w | 815003 w | | | | | | | | |
| Sub-Saharan Africa | 3013 w | .. w | | | | | | | | |
| **East Asia & Pacific** | **34582 w** | **274680 w** | | | | | | | | |
| South Asia | 10545 w | 54788 w | | | | | | | | |
| Europe | .. w | .. w | | | | | | | | |
| Middle East & North Africa | 4813 w | 38858 w | | | | | | | | |
| Latin America & Caribbean | 35434 w | 255504 w | | | | | | | | |
| **EAST ASIA AND PACIFIC** | | | | | | | | | | |
| ***Asian tigers*** | | | | | | | | | | |
| Korea, Rep. | 1880 | 66215 | 26 | 12 | 17 | 14 | 11 | 30 | 11 | 9 |
| Malaysia | 500 | .. | 26 | 18 | 3 | 7 | 8 | 23 | 9 | 14 |
| Thailand | 1130 | 17635 | 43 | 29 * | 13 | 18 * | 9 | 13 * | 6 | 7 * |
| ***Socialist economies in transition*** | | | | | | | | | | |
| Cambodia | .. | .. | .. | .. | .. | .. | .. | .. | .. | .. |
| China | 27555 | 145646 | .. | 12 * | .. | 14 * | .. | 26 * | .. | 12 * |
| Lao P.D.R. | .. | .. | .. | .. | .. | .. | .. | .. | .. | .. |
| Mongolia | .. | .. | .. | .. | .. | .. | .. | .. | .. | .. |
| Myanmar | 225 | 1546 | .. | .. | .. | .. | .. | .. | .. | .. |
| Viet Nam | .. | .. | .. | .. | .. | .. | .. | .. | .. | .. |
| ***Large island economies*** | | | | | | | | | | |
| Indonesia | 994 | 17272 | 65 | .. | 14 | .. | 2 | .. | 6 | .. |
| Papua New Guinea | 35 | 392 | 23 | .. | 1 | .. | 35 | .. | 4 | .. |
| Philippines | 1665 | 10728 | 39 | 41 | 8 | 8 | 8 | 9 | 13 | 10 |

| | | | | | | | | | | |
|---|---|---|---|---|---|---|---|---|---|---|
| ***Pacific island economies*** | | | | | | | | | | |
| Fiji | 27 | 111 | 61 | .. | 2 | .. | 3 | .. | 3 | .. |
| Kiribati | .. | 1 | .. | .. | .. | .. | .. | .. | .. | .. |
| Maldives | .. | .. | .. | .. | .. | .. | .. | .. | .. | .. |
| Solomon Islands | .. | .. | .. | .. | .. | .. | .. | .. | .. | .. |
| Tonga | .. | .. | .. | .. | .. | .. | .. | .. | .. | .. |
| Vanuatu | .. | 8 | .. | .. | .. | .. | .. | .. | .. | .. |
| Western Samoa | .. | .. | .. | .. | .. | .. | .. | .. | .. | .. |
| ***Other*** | | | | | | | | | | |
| Hong Kong | 1013 | 11034 | 4 | 6 | 41 | 38 | 16 | 22 | 2 | 2 |
| Japan | 73339 | 829238 | 8 | 9 | 8 | 5 | 34 | 39 | 11 | 10 |
| Singapore | 379 | 8463 | 12 | 5 | 5 | 4 | 28 | 53 | 4 | 11 |
| **MEMORANDUM ITEMS** | | | | | | | | | | |
| United States | 254115 | .. | 12 | 12 | 8 | 5 | 31 | 32 | 10 | 11 |
| European Community | 245554 w | 1144878 w | | | | | | | | |
| India | 7928 | 44445 | 13 | 11 | 21 | 12 | 20 | 26 | 14 | 17 |
| Bangladesh | 527 | 1730 | 30 | 23 | 47 | 36 | 3 | 5 | 11 | 18 |
| Nigeria | 426 | 2365 * | 36 | .. | 26 | .. | 1 | .. | 6 | .. |
| Tanzania | 118 | 212 | 36 | .. | 28 | .. | 5 | .. | 4 | .. |
| Turkey | 1930 | 18030 | 26 | 17 | 15 | 15 | 8 | 14 | 7 | 14 |
| Hungary | .. | 8724 | 12 | 10 | 13 | 9 | 28 | 29 | 8 | 13 |
| Poland | .. | .. | 20 | 16 | 19 | 16 | 24 | 27 | 8 | 6 |
| Egypt, Arab Rep. | .. | .. | 17 | 31 | 35 | 16 | 9 | 9 | 12 | 8 |
| Argentina | 5523 | .. | 18 | 20 | 17 | 10 | 17 | 13 | 8 | 12 |
| Brazil | 10421 | 120845 | 16 | 12 | 13 | 12 | 22 | 24 | 10 | 12 |
| Chile | 2088 | .. | 17 | 24 | 12 | 7 | 11 | 4 | 5 | 8 |
| Mexico | 8449 | 51138 | 28 | 20 | 15 | 11 | 13 | 14 | 11 | 14 |

# Table 7. Growth of Consumption and Investment

| Country or group | General government consumption 1965–80 | General government consumption 1980–90 | Private consumption, etc. 1965–80 | Private consumption, etc. 1980–90 | Gross domestic investment 1965–80 | Gross domestic investment 1980–90 |
|---|---|---|---|---|---|---|
| | *Average annual growth rate (percent)* | | | | | |
| **GROUP AVERAGES** | | | | | | |
| Low-income economies | 5.8 w | 6.4 w | 4.2 w | 4.7 w | 7.6 w | 7.4 w |
| Middle-income economies | 7.4 w | 3 w | 5.9 w | 2.4 w | 8.6 w | -0.1 w |
| Low-and middle-income econ. | 7 w | 3.9 w | 5.4 w | 3.2 w | 8.3 w | 2.2 w |
| Sub-Saharan Africa | 6.8 w | 1.1 w | 4.1 w | 1 w | 8.7 w | -4.3 w |
| **East Asia & Pacific** | **7.5 w** | **6.2 w** | **6.2 w** | **6.2 w** | **11.1 w** | **10.6 w** |
| South Asia | 4.6 w | 8.5 w | 3.1 w | 5.1 w | 4.1 w | 4.6 w |
| Europe | .. w | 1.8 w | .. w | 2.7 w | .. w | -0.1 w |
| Middle East & North Africa | .. w | .. w | .. w | .. w | .. w | .. w |
| Latin America & Caribbean | 6.5 w | 5.5 w | 5.9 w | 1 w | 8.2 w | -2 w |
| **EAST ASIA AND PACIFIC** | | | | | | |
| ***Asian tigers*** | | | | | | |
| Korea, Rep. | 7.7 | 6 | 8 | 8 | 15.9 | 12.5 |
| Malaysia | 8.5 | 2.7 | 6.2 | 4.2 | 10.4 | 2.9 |
| Thailand | 9.5 | 4.3 | 6.4 | 6.5 | 8 | 8.7 |
| ***Socialist economies in transition*** | | | | | | |
| Cambodia | .. | .. | .. | .. | .. | .. |
| China | 6.2 | 9.5 | 6 | 6.8 | 10.7 | 13.7 |
| Lao P.D.R. | .. | .. | .. | .. | .. | .. |
| Mongolia | .. | .. | .. | .. | .. | .. |
| Myanmar | a | a | 3.5 | 0.8 | 5.6 | -3.4 |
| Viet Nam | .. | .. | .. | .. | .. | .. |
| ***Large island economies*** | | | | | | |
| Indonesia | 11.4 | 4.6 | 5.2 | 4.5 | 16.1 | 7.1 |
| Papua New Guinea | 0.1 | -0.3 | 5.3 | 1 | 1.4 | -1.7 |
| Philippines | 7.7 | 0.4 | 5.2 | 2.4 | 7.6 | -2.5 |

| | | | | | | |
|---|---|---|---|---|---|---|
| ***Pacific island economies*** | | | | | | |
| Fiji | 8.5 | 0.6 | 6.9 | 3.4 | 6.8 | -6.6 |
| Kiribati | .. | .. | .. | .. | .. | .. |
| Maldives | .. | .. | .. | .. | .. | .. |
| Solomon Islands | .. | 5.6 * | .. | 5.1 * | .. | 3.5 * |
| Tonga | .. | .. | .. | .. | .. | .. |
| Vanuatu | .. | .. | .. | .. | .. | .. |
| Western Samoa | .. | -3.3 | .. | 3.3 | .. | -2 |
| ***Other*** | | | | | | |
| Hong Kong | 7.7 | 5.3 | 9 | 6.8 | 8.6 | 3.6 |
| Japan | 5.3 | 2.4 | 6.2 | 3.7 | 6.9 | 5.7 |
| Singapore | 10.2 | 6.6 | .. | 5.9 | 13.3 | 3.6 |
| **MEMORANDUM ITEMS** | | | | | | |
| United States | 1.3 | 3.3 | 3.3 | 3.4 | 2.1 | 4.4 |
| European Community | 3.4 w | 1.8 w | 3.9 w | 2.6 w | 2.5 w | 3.1 w |
| India | 4.7 | 7.8 | 3.1 | 5.3 | 4.3 | 5 |
| Bangladesh | .. | .. | 2 | 3.7 | 0 | -0.6 |
| Nigeria | 13.9 | -3.6 | 6.2 | -3.3 | 14.7 | -10.2 |
| Tanzania | a | 8.4 * | 4.5 | 3.3 * | 6.2 | 0.3 * |
| Turkey | 6.1 | 3.1 | 5.4 | 5.9 | 8.8 | 3.8 |
| Hungary | .. | 2.1 | .. | 0.8 | 9.1 | -0.8 |
| Poland | .. | 1 | .. | 1.3 | .. | 1 |
| Egypt, Arab Rep. | a | 2.2 | 6.7 | 3.4 | 11.3 | 0.2 |
| Argentina | 3.2 | 5.4 | 2.9 | -2.7 | 4.6 | -8.3 |
| Brazil | 6.8 | 8.8 | 8.7 | 1.7 | 11.3 | 0.2 |
| Chile | 4 | -0.1 | 0.9 | 1.7 | 0.5 | 4.3 |
| Mexico | 8.5 | 1.9 | 5.9 | 1.1 | 8.5 | -3.4 |

a. General government consumption figures are not available separately; they are included in Private consumption, etc.

# Table 8. Structure of Demand

| | Distribution of gross domestic product (percent) | | | | | | | | | |
|---|---|---|---|---|---|---|---|---|---|---|
| | *General government consumption* | | *Private consumption, etc.* | | *Gross domestic investment* | | *Gross domestic savings* | | *Exports of goods and nonfactor services* | |
| *Country or group* | *1965* | *1990* | *1965* | *1990* | *1965* | *1990* | *1965* | *1990* | *1965* | *1990* |
| **GROUP AVERAGES** | | | | | | | | | | |
| Low-income economies | 9 w | 11 w | 74 w | 65 w | 19 w | 31 w | 18 w | 30 w | 8 w | 18 w |
| Middle-income economies | 11 w | 14 w | 67 w | 63 w | 21 w | 23 w | 22 w | 23 w | 18 w | .. w |
| Low-and middle-income econ. | 10 w | 13 w | 70 w | 63 w | 20 w | 26 w | 20 w | 25 w | 13 w | 24 w |
| Sub-Saharan Africa | 11 w | 15 w | 77 w | 69 w | 15 w | 16 w | 13 w | 16 w | 22 w | 29 w |
| **East Asia & Pacific** | **8 w** | **10 w** | **69 w** | **55 w** | **22 w** | **37 w** | **22 w** | **35 w** | **8 w** | **31 w** |
| South Asia | 9 w | 12 w | 77 w | 68 w | 17 w | 21 w | 14 w | 17 w | 6 w | 9 w |
| Europe | .. w | 14 w | .. w | 65 w | .. w | 25 w | .. w | 21 w | .. w | 29 w |
| Middle East & North Africa | 15 w | .. w | 60 w | .. w | 17 w | .. w | 22 w | .. w | 26 w | .. w |
| Latin America & Caribbean | 9 w | 13 w | 70 w | 66 w | 21 w | 19 w | 21 w | 21 w | 14 w | 16 w |
| **EAST ASIA AND PACIFIC** | | | | | | | | | | |
| ***Asian tigers*** | | | | | | | | | | |
| Korea, Rep. | 9 | a | 83 | 63 | 15 | 37 | 8 | .. | 9 | 32 |
| Malaysia | 15 | 13 | 61 | 54 | 20 | 34 | 24 | 33 | 42 | 79 |
| Thailand | 10 | 10 | 72 | 57 | 20 | 37 | 19 | 34 | 16 | 38 |
| ***Socialist economies in transition*** | | | | | | | | | | |
| Cambodia | 16 | .. | 71 | .. | 13 | .. | 12 | .. | 12 | .. |
| China | 8 | 8 | 68 | 49 | 24 | 39 | 25 | 43 | 4 | 18 |
| Lao P.D.R. | .. | 12 | .. | 89 | .. | 12 | .. | -2 | .. | 10 |
| Mongolia | .. | 24 | .. | 73 | .. | 30 | .. | 3 | .. | 23 |
| Myanmar | a | a | 87 | 89 | 19 | 14 | 13 | .. | 14 | 3 |
| Viet Nam | .. | .. | .. | .. | .. | .. | .. | .. | .. | .. |
| ***Large island economies*** | | | | | | | | | | |
| Indonesia | 5 | 9 | 87 | 54 | 8 | 36 | 8 | 37 | 5 | 26 |
| Papua New Guinea | 34 | 24 | 64 | 66 | 22 | 25 | 2 | 10 | 18 | 37 |
| Philippines | 9 | 9 | 70 | 75 | 21 | 22 | 21 | 16 | 17 | 28 |

| | | | | | | | | | | |
|---|---|---|---|---|---|---|---|---|---|---|
| ***Pacific island economies*** | | | | | | | | | | |
| Fiji | 13 | 16 | 75 | 67 | 20 | 19 | 12 | 17 | 46 | 63 |
| Kiribati | .. | .. | .. | .. | .. | .. | .. | .. | .. | .. |
| Maldives | .. | .. | .. | .. | .. | .. | .. | .. | .. | .. |
| Solomon Islands | .. | .. | .. | .. | .. | .. | .. | .. | .. | .. |
| Tonga | .. | .. | .. | .. | .. | .. | .. | .. | .. | .. |
| Vanuatu | .. | .. | .. | .. | .. | .. | .. | .. | .. | .. |
| Western Samoa | .. | 22 | .. | 101 | .. | 41 | .. | -23 | .. | 19 |
| ***Other*** | | | | | | | | | | |
| Hong Kong | 7 | 8 | 64 | 59 | 36 | 28 | 29 | 33 | 71 | 137 |
| Japan | 8 | 9 | 59 | 57 | 32 | 33 | 33 | 34 | 11 | 11 |
| Singapore | 10 | 11 | 80 | 45 | 22 | 39 | 10 | 45 | 123 | 190 |
| **MEMORANDUM ITEMS** | | | | | | | | | | |
| United States | 17 | 18 | 63 | 67 | 20 | 16 | 21 | 15 | 5 | 10 |
| European Community | 15 w | 18 w | 61 w | 60 w | 25 w | 21 w | 25 w | 22 w | 19 w | 29 w |
| India | 9 | 12 | 76 | 68 | 17 | 23 | 15 | 20 | 4 | 8 |
| Bangladesh | 9 | 9 | 83 | 89 | 11 | 12 | 8 | 2 | 10 | 8 |
| Nigeria | 7 | 11 | 83 | 59 | 15 | 15 | 10 | 29 | 11 | 39 |
| Tanzania | 10 | .. | 74 | .. | 15 | .. | 16 | .. | 26 | .. |
| Turkey | 12 | 14 | 74 | 68 | 15 | 23 | 13 | 18 | 6 | 19 |
| Hungary | a | 11 | 75 | 62 | 26 | 23 | .. | 27 | .. | 33 |
| Poland | .. | 7 | .. | 54 | .. | 31 | .. | 39 | .. | 26 |
| Egypt, Arab Rep. | 19 | 10 | 67 | 80 | 18 | 23 | 14 | 10 | 18 | 20 |
| Argentina | 8 | 4 | 69 | 80 | 19 | 8 | 22 | 16 | 8 | 14 |
| Brazil | 11 | 16 | 67 | 61 | 20 | 22 | 22 | 23 | 8 | 7 |
| Chile | 11 | 10 | 73 | 67 | 15 | 20 | 16 | 23 | 14 | 37 |
| Mexico | 6 | 11 | 75 | 70 | 20 | 20 | 19 | 19 | 8 | 16 |

a. General government consumption figures are not available separately; they are included in Private consumption, etc.

## Table 9. Central Government Expenditure

| Country or group | Defense 1972 | Defense 1990 | Education 1972 | Education 1990 | Health 1972 | Health 1990 | Housing amenities; social security and welfare 1972 | Housing amenities; social security and welfare 1990 | Economic services 1972 | Economic services 1990 |
|---|---|---|---|---|---|---|---|---|---|---|
| | *Percentage of total expenditure* | | | | | | | | | |
| **GROUP AVERAGES** | | | | | | | | | | |
| Low-income economies | | | | | | | | | | |
| Middle-income economies | | | | | | | | | | |
| Low-and middle-income econ. | | | | | | | | | | |
| Sub-Saharan Africa | | | | | | | | | | |
| **East Asia & Pacific** | | | | | | | | | | |
| South Asia | | | | | | | | | | |
| Europe | | | | | | | | | | |
| Middle East & North Africa | | | | | | | | | | |
| Latin America & Caribbean | | | | | | | | | | |
| **EAST ASIA AND PACIFIC** | | | | | | | | | | |
| ***Asian tigers*** | | | | | | | | | | |
| Korea, Rep. | 25.8 | 25.8 | 15.8 | 19.6 | 1.2 | 2.2 | 5.9 | 12.2 | 25.6 | 17 |
| Malaysia | 18.5 | 8.6 | 23.4 | 0 | 6.8 | 0 | 4.4 | 5.5 | 14.2 | 20.6 |
| Thailand | 20.2 | 17.3 | 19.9 | 20.1 | 3.7 | 6.8 | 7 | 5.8 | 25.6 | 22.1 |
| ***Socialist economies in transition*** | | | | | | | | | | |
| Cambodia | .. | .. | .. | .. | .. | .. | .. | .. | .. | .. |
| China | .. | .. | .. | .. | .. | .. | .. | .. | .. | .. |
| Lao P.D.R. | .. | .. | .. | .. | .. | .. | .. | .. | .. | .. |
| Mongolia | .. | .. | .. | .. | .. | .. | .. | .. | .. | .. |
| Myanmar | 31.6 * | 24.7 * | 15 * | 16.8 * | 6.1 * | 4.6 * | 7.5 * | 15.4 * | 20.1 * | 20.5 * |
| Viet Nam | .. | .. | .. | .. | .. | .. | .. | .. | .. | .. |
| ***Large island economies*** | | | | | | | | | | |
| Indonesia | 18.6 * | 8 * | 7.4 * | 8.4 * | 1.4 * | 2 * | 0.9 * | 1.5 * | 30.5 * | 27.6 * |
| Papua New Guinea | .. | 4.7 * | .. | 15.3 * | .. | 9.4 * | .. | 3.1 * | .. | 20.8 * |
| Philippines | 10.9 | 11 | 16.3 | 16.9 | 3.2 | 4.1 | 4.3 | 2.3 | 17.6 | 23.6 |

| | | | | | | | | | | |
|---|---|---|---|---|---|---|---|---|---|---|
| ***Pacific island economies*** | | | | | | | | | | |
| Fiji | 1.1 | 8.7 | 19.9 | 21 | 13.3 | 7.7 | 6.6 | 6.9 | 25.5 | 21.5 |
| Kiribati | .. | .. | .. | .. | .. | .. | .. | .. | .. | .. |
| Maldives | .. | 0 | .. | 14.3 | .. | 18.4 | .. | 6.9 | .. | 22.8 |
| Solomon Islands | .. | 0 * | .. | 22.4 * | .. | 6.2 * | .. | 3.4 * | .. | 34.7 * |
| Tonga | .. | 0 | .. | 11.1 | .. | 7 | .. | 8 | .. | 42.5 |
| Vanuatu | .. | 0 | .. | 14.8 | .. | 7.6 | .. | 0.1 | .. | 50 |
| Western Samoa | .. | .. | .. | .. | .. | .. | .. | .. | .. | .. |
| ***Other*** | | | | | | | | | | |
| Hong Kong | .. | .. | .. | .. | .. | .. | .. | .. | .. | .. |
| Japan | .. | .. | .. | .. | .. | .. | .. | .. | .. | .. |
| Singapore | 35.3 | 21.6 * | 15.7 | 18.1 * | 7.8 | 4.7 * | 3.9 | 11.7 * | 9.9 | 20 * |
| **MEMORANDUM ITEMS** | | | | | | | | | | |
| United States | 32.2 | 22.6 | 3.2 | 1.7 | 8.6 | 13.5 | 35.3 | 28.2 | 10.6 | 10.2 |
| European Community | .. w | .. w | .. w | .. w | .. w | .. w | .. w | .. w | .. w | .. w |
| India | 26.2 * | 17 | 2.3 * | 2.5 | 1.5 * | 1.6 | 3.2 * | 6.9 | 19.9 * | 20.8 |
| Bangladesh | 5.1 * | 10.1 * | 14.8 * | 11.2 * | 5 * | 4.8 * | 9.8 * | 8 * | 39.3 * | 34.4 * |
| Nigeria | 40.2 | .. | 4.5 | .. | 3.6 | .. | 0.8 | .. | 19.6 | .. |
| Tanzania | 11.9 | .. | 17.3 | .. | 7.2 | .. | 2.1 | .. | 39 | .. |
| Turkey | 15.5 | 11.7 | 18.1 | 19.2 | 3.2 | 3.6 | 3.1 | 3.6 | 42 | 17.8 |
| Hungary | .. | 3.6 | .. | 3.3 | .. | 7.9 | .. | 35.3 | .. | 22 |
| Poland | .. | .. | .. | .. | .. | .. | .. | .. | .. | .. |
| Egypt, Arab Rep. | .. | 12.7 * | .. | 13.4 * | .. | 2.8 * | .. | 17.8 * | .. | 8.2 * |
| Argentina | .. | 8.6 * | .. | 9.3 * | .. | 2 * | .. | 40.9 * | .. | 20.5 * |
| Brazil | 0 | 4.2 * | 0 | 5.3 * | 0 | 7.2 * | 0 | 20.1 * | 0 | 6.9 * |
| Chile | 10 | 8.4 * | 20 | 10.1 * | 10 | 5.9 * | 40 | 33.9 * | 0 | 8.8 * |
| Mexico | 4.5 | 2.4 | 16.4 | 13.9 | 4.5 | 1.9 | 25.4 | 13 | 35.8 | 13.4 |

# Table 10. Central Government Current Revenue

| | Percentage of total current tax revenue | | | | | | | | | |
|---|---|---|---|---|---|---|---|---|---|---|
| | *Taxes on income, profit and capital gain* | | *Social security contributions* | | *Domestic taxes on goods and services* | | *Taxes on international trade and transactions* | | *Other taxes* | |
| *Country or group* | *1972* | *1990* | *1972* | *1990* | *1972* | *1990* | *1972* | *1990* | *1972* | *1990* |
| **GROUP AVERAGES** | | | | | | | | | | |
| Low-income economies | | | | | | | | | | |
| Middle-income economies | | | | | | | | | | |
| Low-and middle-income econ. | | | | | | | | | | |
| Sub-Saharan Africa | | | | | | | | | | |
| **East Asia & Pacific** | | | | | | | | | | |
| South Asia | | | | | | | | | | |
| Europe | | | | | | | | | | |
| Middle East & North Africa | | | | | | | | | | |
| Latin America & Caribbean | | | | | | | | | | |
| **EAST ASIA AND PACIFIC** | | | | | | | | | | |
| ***Asian tigers*** | | | | | | | | | | |
| Korea, Rep. | 29 | 34 | 0.7 | 4.9 | 41.7 | 33.5 | 10.7 | 10.6 | 5.3 | 5.7 |
| Malaysia | 25.2 | 30.5 | 0.1 | 0.8 | 24.2 | 24.3 | 27.9 | 16.7 | 1.4 | 2.5 |
| Thailand | 12.1 | 24.2 | 0 | 0.1 | 46.3 | 41.4 | 28.7 | 22.1 | 1.8 | 4.3 |
| ***Socialist economies in transition*** | | | | | | | | | | |
| Cambodia | .. | .. | .. | .. | .. | .. | .. | .. | .. | .. |
| China | .. | .. | .. | .. | .. | .. | .. | .. | .. | .. |
| Lao P.D.R. | .. | .. | .. | .. | .. | .. | .. | .. | .. | .. |
| Mongolia | .. | .. | .. | .. | .. | .. | .. | .. | .. | .. |
| Myanmar | 28.7 * | 9 * | 0 * | 0 * | 34.2 * | 30.7 * | 13.4 * | 14.9 * | 0 * | 0 * |
| Viet Nam | .. | .. | .. | .. | .. | .. | .. | .. | .. | .. |
| ***Large island economies*** | | | | | | | | | | |
| Indonesia | 45.5 | 57.5 * | 0 | 0 * | 22.8 | 25.1 * | 17.6 | 6 * | 3.5 | 3 * |
| Papua New Guinea | .. | 44.6 * | .. | 0 * | .. | 10.5 * | .. | 24.9 * | .. | 1.8 * |
| Philippines | 13.8 | 28.3 | 0 | 0 | 24.3 | 30.7 | 23 | 25.1 | 29.7 | 2.9 |

| | | | | | | | | | | |
|---|---|---|---|---|---|---|---|---|---|---|
| ***Pacific island economies*** | | | | | | | | | | |
| Fiji | 34.3 | 37.2 | 0 | 0 | 11.5 | 14.6 | 41 | 32.2 | -0.5 | 1 |
| Kiribati | .. | .. | .. | .. | .. | .. | .. | .. | .. | .. |
| Maldives | .. | 1.2 | .. | 0 | .. | 20 | .. | 34.6 | .. | 4.2 |
| Solomon Islands | .. | 31.7 | .. | 0 | .. | 3.4 | .. | 53.7 | .. | -0.6 |
| Tonga | .. | 10 | .. | 0 | .. | 0 | .. | 50.2 | .. | 7.7 |
| Vanuatu | .. | 0 | .. | 0 | .. | 25.9 | .. | 56.5 | .. | 0 |
| Western Samoa | .. | .. | .. | .. | .. | .. | .. | .. | .. | .. |
| ***Other*** | | | | | | | | | | |
| Hong Kong | .. | .. | .. | .. | .. | .. | .. | .. | .. | .. |
| Japan | 64.8 | 71.2 * | 0 | 0 * | 22.6 | 12 * | 3.5 | 1.3 * | 6.8 | 9.9 * |
| Singapore | 24.4 | 24.3 * | 0 | 0 * | 17.6 | 19.6 * | 11.1 | 2.5 * | 15.5 | 14.9 * |
| **MEMORANDUM ITEMS** | | | | | | | | | | |
| United States | 59.4 | 51.6 | 23.6 | 34.6 | 7.1 | 3.2 | 1.6 | 1.6 | 2.5 | 1.1 |
| European Community | 24.3 w | 27.7 w | 33.5 w | 35.8 w | 30.7 w | 27.7 w | 1.5 w | .. w | 3.5 w | 2 w |
| India | 21.3 * | 15.4 | 0 * | 0 | 44.5 * | 35.5 | 20.1 * | 28.8 | 0.9 * | 0.4 |
| Bangladesh | 3.7 * | 8.6 * | 0 * | 0 * | 22.4 * | 25.8 * | 18 * | 27.3 * | 3.8 * | 15.2 * |
| Nigeria | 43 | .. | 0 | .. | 26.3 | .. | 17.5 | .. | 0.2 | .. |
| Tanzania | 29.9 | .. | 0 | .. | 29.1 | .. | 21.7 | .. | 0.5 | .. |
| Turkey | 30.8 | 43.3 | 0 | 0 | 31 | 32.1 | 14.6 | 6.2 | 6.1 | 3 |
| Hungary | .. | 17.9 | .. | 29.2 | .. | 31.3 | .. | 5.8 | .. | 0.2 |
| Poland | .. | 30.4 * | .. | 21.4 * | .. | 30.4 * | .. | 6.2 * | .. | 6.5 * |
| Egypt, Arab Rep. | .. | 15.9 * | .. | 14.2 * | .. | 11.9 * | .. | 14 * | .. | 8.2 * |
| Argentina | .. | 4.3 * | .. | 43.4 * | .. | 22.4 * | .. | 11.4 * | .. | 10.3 * |
| Brazil | .. | 5 * | .. | 6 * | .. | 3.9 * | .. | 0.6 * | .. | 0.8 * |
| Chile | 14.3 | 23.3 * | 28.6 | 6 * | 28.6 | 37.1 * | 14.3 | 9.8 * | 0 | -0.2 * |
| Mexico | 37.3 | 36.5 | 18.6 | 13.6 | 32.2 | 56 | 13.6 | 4.6 | -8.5 | -18.3 |

# Table 11. Money and Interest Rates

| | Monetary holdings, broadly defined | | | | | Average annual inflation (GDP deflator) | Nominal interest rates of banks (average annual percentage) | | | |
|---|---|---|---|---|---|---|---|---|---|---|
| | Average annual nominal growth rate (percent) | | Average outstanding as a percentage of GDP | | | | Deposit rate | | Lending rate | |
| Country or group | 1965–80 | 1980–90 | 1965 | 1980 | 1990 | 1980–90 | 1980 | 1990 | 1980 | 1990 |
| **GROUP AVERAGES** | | | | | | | | | | |
| Low-income economies | | | | | | | | | | |
| Middle-income economies | | | | | | | | | | |
| Low-and middle-income econ. | | | | | | | | | | |
| Sub-Saharan Africa | | | | | | | | | | |
| **East Asia & Pacific** | | | | | | | | | | |
| South Asia | | | | | | | | | | |
| Europe | | | | | | | | | | |
| Middle East & North Africa | | | | | | | | | | |
| Latin America & Caribbean | | | | | | | | | | |
| **EAST ASIA AND PACIFIC** | | | | | | | | | | |
| ***Asian tigers*** | | | | | | | | | | |
| Korea, Rep. | 35.5 | 21 | 11.1 | 31.7 | 53.2 | 5.1 | 19.5 | 10 | 18 | 10 |
| Malaysia | 21.5 | 12.6 * | 26.3 | 69.8 | .. | 1.6 | 6.23 | 5.9 | 7.75 | 7.17 |
| Thailand | 17.9 | 18.8 | 23.6 | 37.4 | 71.5 | 3.3 | 12 | 12.25 | 18 | 15 * |
| ***Socialist economies in transition*** | | | | | | | | | | |
| Cambodia | .. | .. | .. | .. | .. | .. | .. | .. | .. | .. |
| China | .. | 25.4 | .. | 33.6 | 74.7 | 5.8 | 5.4 | .. | 5.04 | 11.15 * |
| Lao P.D.R. | .. | .. | .. | .. | .. | .. | 7.2 | .. | 4.8 | .. |
| Mongolia | .. | .. | .. | .. | .. | -1.3 | .. | .. | .. | .. |
| Myanmar | 11.5 | 11.2 * | 29 | 23.9 | .. | 11.4 | 1.5 | 1.5 * | 8 | 8 * |
| Viet Nam | .. | .. | .. | .. | .. | .. | .. | .. | .. | .. |
| ***Large island economies*** | | | | | | | | | | |
| Indonesia | 54.4 | 25.8 | .. | 13.2 | 36.2 | 8.4 | 6 | 17.3 | .. | 20.61 |
| Papua New Guinea | .. | 8 | .. | 32.9 | 34 | 5.3 | 6.9 | 8.67 | 11.15 | 15.52 |
| Philippines | .. | .. | .. | .. | .. | 14.9 | 12.25 | 19.54 | 14 | 24.12 |

| | | | | | | | | | | |
|---|---|---|---|---|---|---|---|---|---|---|
| ***Pacific island economies*** | | | | | | | | | | |
| Fiji | 17.2 | 10.9 | 34.3 | 32.2 | 43.6 | 6.1 | 4.5 | 4 | 12 | 11.86 |
| Kiribati | .. | .. | .. | .. | .. | 5.5 | .. | .. | .. | .. |
| Maldives | .. | 17.2 | .. | .. | 56.4 | 4.5 * | 6 | .. | .. | .. |
| Solomon Islands | .. | 16.7 | .. | 40.8 | 31.3 | 10 | .. | 10.5 | .. | 18 |
| Tonga | .. | 14.4 * | .. | .. | 36.6 | 7 * | 6.25 | 7.25 | 10 | 13.5 |
| Vanuatu | .. | 16.5 | .. | 73 | .. | 4.8 * | .. | 7 | .. | 17.33 |
| Western Samoa | 15.4 | 17.1 | .. | 17.5 | 42.8 | 9.2 | 6.5 | 8.25 | .. | 13.25 |
| ***Other*** | | | | | | | | | | |
| Hong Kong | .. | .. | .. | 69.3 | .. | 7.2 | .. | .. | .. | .. |
| Japan | 17.2 | 9 | 106.7 | 134 | 183.1 | 1.5 | 5.5 | 4.08 | 8.35 | 6.95 |
| Singapore | 17.6 | 13.3 | 58.4 | 74.4 | 121.9 | 1.7 | 9.37 | 4.67 | 11.72 | 7.36 |
| **MEMORANDUM ITEMS** | | | | | | | | | | |
| United States | 9.2 | 8.4 | 63.8 | 58.8 | 66.6 | 3.7 | .. | .. | 15.27 | 10.01 |
| European Community | | | | | | | | | | |
| India | 15.3 | 16.7 | 23.7 | 36.2 | 44.7 | 7.9 | .. | .. | 16.5 | 16.5 |
| Bangladesh | .. | 21.6 | .. | 16.7 | 28.3 | 9.6 | 8.25 | 12 * | 11.33 | 16 |
| Nigeria | 28.5 | 14.1 | 10.7 | 23.8 | 17.6 | 18.2 | 5.27 | .. | 8.43 | .. |
| Tanzania | 19.7 * | 21.5 * | .. | 37.2 | .. | 25.7 | 4 | 17 * | 11.5 | 31 * |
| Turkey | 27.5 | 51.9 | 23 | 17.2 | 21.3 | 43.2 | 8 | 47.6 | 25.67 | .. |
| Hungary | .. | .. | .. | .. | .. | 9 | 3 | 23 | 9 | 28 |
| Poland | .. | 51.5 | .. | 58.4 | 22.4 | 54.3 | 3 | 27.8 | 8 | 101.42 |
| Egypt, Arab Rep. | 17.7 | 21.9 | 35.3 | 52.2 | 93.2 | 11.9 | 8.33 | 12 | 13.33 | 19 |
| Argentina | 86.6 | 368.5 | 18.1 | 22.2 | 7.6 | 395.1 | 79.4 | 1585.96 | .. | 796725 * |
| Brazil | -22 | .. | 20621.3 | 18.4 | .. | 284.4 | 115 | 9387.5 | .. | .. |
| Chile | .. | 30.3 * | 16.3 | 21 | .. | 20.5 | 37.46 | 40.27 | 47.14 | 48.83 |
| Mexico | 21.9 | 62.4 | 25.1 | 27.5 | 20.4 | 70.4 | 20.63 | 31.24 | 28.1 | .. |

# Table 12. Growth of Merchandise Trade

| | Merchandise trade (millions of dollars) | | Annual growth rate[a] (percent) | | | | Terms of trade (1987 = 100) | |
|---|---|---|---|---|---|---|---|---|
| | Exports | Imports | Exports | | Imports | | | |
| Country or group | 1990 | 1990 | 1965–80 | 1980–90 | 1965–80 | 1980–90 | 1985 | 1990 |
| **GROUP AVERAGES** | | | | | | | | |
| Low-income economies | 141181 t | 144431 t | 5 w | 5.4 w | 4.5 w | 2.7 w | 107 m | 100 m |
| Middle-income economies | 491128 t | 485897 t | 3.9 w | 3.8 w | 6.1 w | 0.9 w | 110 m | 102 m |
| Low-and middle-income econ. | 632309 t | 630328 t | 4.1 w | 4.1 w | 5.7 w | 1.4 w | 109 m | 100 m |
| Sub-Saharan Africa | 34062 t | 32377 t | 5.9 w | 0.3 w | 4.9 w | -4.4 w | 110 m | 100 m |
| **East Asia & Pacific** | **217030 t** | **224021 t** | **8.5 w** | **9.8 w** | **7.1 w** | **8 w** | **106 m** | **103 m** |
| South Asia | 27699 t | 38217 t | 1.8 w | 6.8 w | 0.6 w | 4.1 w | 101 m | 95 m |
| Europe | 94082 t | 126493 t | .. w | .. w | .. w | .. w | 94 m | 103 m |
| Middle East & North Africa | 112644 t | 89842 t | 5.7 w | -1.1 w | 12.8 w | -4.7 w | 130 m | 96 m |
| Latin America & Caribbean | 123181 t | 101119 t | -1 w | 3 w | 4.1 w | -2.1 w | 111 m | 110 m |
| **EAST ASIA AND PACIFIC** | | | | | | | | |
| ***Asian tigers*** | | | | | | | | |
| Korea, Rep. | 64837 | 69585 | 27.2 | 12.8 | 15.2 | 10.8 | 103 | 108 |
| Malaysia | 29409 | 29251 | 4.6 | 10.3 | 2.2 | 5.6 | 117 | 94 |
| Thailand | 23002 | 33129 | 8.6 | 13.2 | 4.1 | 10.2 | 91 | 99 |
| ***Socialist economies in transition*** | | | | | | | | |
| Cambodia | .. | .. | .. | .. | .. | .. | .. | .. |
| China | 62091 | 53345 | 4.8 | 11 | 7.4 | 9.8 | 109 | 111 |
| Lao P.D.R. | .. | .. | .. | .. | .. | .. | .. | .. |
| Mongolia | .. | .. | .. | .. | .. | .. | .. | .. |
| Myanmar | 322 | 270 | -2.1 | -10.1 | -4.4 | -14.5 | 106 | 127 |
| Viet Nam | .. | .. | .. | .. | .. | .. | .. | .. |
| ***Large island economies*** | | | | | | | | |
| Indonesia | 25553 | 21837 | 9.6 | 2.8 | 13 | 1.4 | 134 | 111 |
| Papua New Guinea | 1140 | 1288 | 13 | 6.2 | 1.6 | 2.6 | 111 | 75 |
| Philippines | 8681 | 13080 | 4.6 | 2.5 | 2.9 | 2.3 | 93 | 93 |

| | | | | | | | | |
|---|---|---|---|---|---|---|---|---|
| ***Pacific island economies*** | | | | | | | | |
| Fiji | 531 | 741 | -2.4 | 13 | 2.4 | -0.5 | 94 | 130 |
| Kiribati | .. | .. | .. | .. | .. | .. | .. | .. |
| Maldives | .. | .. | .. | .. | .. | .. | .. | .. |
| Solomon Islands | 70 | 92 | .. | .. | .. | .. | .. | .. |
| Tonga | 12 | 62 | .. | .. | .. | .. | .. | .. |
| Vanuatu | .. | .. | .. | .. | .. | .. | .. | .. |
| Western Samoa | 9 | 85 | .. | .. | .. | .. | .. | .. |
| ***Other*** | | | | | | | | |
| Hong Kong | 29002 | 82495 | 9.1 | 6.2 * | 8.3 | 11 * | 97 | 100 * |
| Japan | 286768 | 231223 | 11.4 | 4.2 | 4.9 | 5.6 | 71 | 91 |
| Singapore | 52627 | 60647 | 4.7 | 8.6 | 7 | 6.7 | 99 | 100 |
| **MEMORANDUM ITEMS** | | | | | | | | |
| United States | 371466 | 515635 | 6.4 | 3.3 | 5.5 | 7.6 | 100 | 100 |
| European Community | 1349971 t | 1405271 t | 7.3 w | 4.1 w | 3.9 w | 4.2 w | 94 m | 102 m |
| India | 17967 | 23692 | 3 | 6.5 | 1.2 | 4.2 | 96 | 96 |
| Bangladesh | 1674 | 3646 | .. | 7.6 | .. | 8 | 109 | 95 |
| Nigeria | 13671 | 5688 | 11.1 | -1.6 | 14.6 | -15.1 | 167 | 100 |
| Tanzania | 300 | 935 | -4.2 | -7.4 * | 1.6 | -0.5 * | 101 | 108 * |
| Turkey | 12959 | 22300 | 5.5 | 9.1 | 7.7 | 7 | 82 | 98 |
| Hungary | 9588 | 8646 | .. | 5.5 | .. | 1.3 | 104 | 87 |
| Poland | 13627 | 9781 | .. | 3 | .. | 1.2 | 94 | 103 |
| Egypt, Arab Rep. | 2985 | 10340 | -0.1 | 2.1 | 3.6 | -1.7 | 131 | 76 |
| Argentina | 12353 | 4077 | 4.7 | 1.4 | 1.8 | -8.4 | 110 | 112 |
| Brazil | 31243 | 22459 | 9.3 | 4 | 8.2 | -0.3 | 92 | 123 |
| Chile | 8579 | 7023 | 8 | 4.8 | 1.4 | 0.6 | 102 | 131 |
| Mexico | 26714 | 28063 | 7.7 | 3.4 | 5.7 | -1.1 | 133 | 110 |

a. For details on how the growth rate is calculated, see World Bank 1992e, p. 293.

# Table 13. Structure of Merchandise Imports

| | Percentage share of merchandise imports | | | | | | | | | |
|---|---|---|---|---|---|---|---|---|---|---|
| | Food | | Fuels | | Other primary commodities | | Machinery and tranport equipment | | Other manufactures | |
| *Country or group* | *1965* | *1990* | *1965* | *1990* | *1965* | *1990* | *1965* | *1990* | *1965* | *1990* |
| **GROUP AVERAGES** | | | | | | | | | | |
| Low-income economies | 17 w | 11 w | 5 w | 8 w | 8 w | 8 w | 33 w | 35 w | 37 w | 37 w |
| Middle-income economies | 15 w | 11 w | 10 w | 12 w | 11 w | 8 w | 30 w | 34 w | 34 w | 35 w |
| Low-and middle-income econ. | 15 w | 11 w | 9 w | 11 w | 10 w | 8 w | 31 w | 34 w | 35 w | 35 w |
| Sub-Saharan Africa | 15 w | 16 w | 7 w | 14 w | 3 w | 4 w | 30 w | 29 w | 45 w | 37 w |
| **East Asia & Pacific** | **13 w** | **7 w** | **6 w** | **9 w** | **9 w** | **10 w** | **32 w** | **38 w** | **40 w** | **35 w** |
| South Asia | 25 w | 12 w | 4 w | 15 w | 11 w | 9 w | 34 w | 28 w | 27 w | 35 w |
| Europe | 14 w | 11 w | 12 w | 17 w | 17 w | 9 w | 32 w | 34 w | 28 w | 34 w |
| Middle East & North Africa | 24 w | 17 w | 5 w | 6 w | 7 w | 6 w | 24 w | 33 w | 40 w | 37 w |
| Latin America & Caribbean | 12 w | 12 w | 13 w | 13 w | 8 w | 7 w | 32 w | 31 w | 35 w | 35 w |
| **EAST ASIA AND PACIFIC** | | | | | | | | | | |
| Asian tigers | | | | | | | | | | |
| Korea, Rep. | 15 | 5 | 7 | 16 | 26 | 15 | 13 | 34 | 38 | 29 |
| Malaysia | 25 | 11 | 12 | 5 | 10 | 6 | 22 | 45 | 32 | 33 |
| Thailand | 6 | 5 | 9 | 9 | 6 | 8 | 31 | 41 | 49 | 37 |
| ***Socialist economies in transition*** | | | | | | | | | | |
| Cambodia | 6 | .. | 7 | .. | 2 | .. | 26 | .. | 58 | .. |
| China | 7 | 8 | 1 | 2 | 10 | 9 | 39 | 41 | 43 | 39 |
| Lao P.D.R. | 27 | .. | 14 | .. | 6 | .. | 19 | .. | 34 | .. |
| Mongolia | .. | .. | .. | .. | .. | .. | .. | .. | .. | .. |
| Myanmar | 15 | 9 | 4 | 3 | 5 | 2 | 18 | 40 | 58 | 46 |
| Viet Nam | .. | .. | .. | .. | .. | .. | .. | .. | .. | .. |
| ***Large island economies*** | | | | | | | | | | |
| Indonesia | 6 | 5 | 3 | 9 | 2 | 9 | 39 | 43 | 50 | 35 |
| Papua New Guinea | 23 | 17 | 4 | 8 | 3 | 2 | 25 | 40 | 45 | 34 |
| Philippines | 20 | 10 | 10 | 13 | 7 | 7 | 33 | 20 | 30 | 50 |

| | | | | | | | | | | |
|---|---|---|---|---|---|---|---|---|---|---|
| ***Pacific island economies*** | | | | | | | | | | |
| Fiji | 24 | 20 | 10 | 16 | 4 | 2 | 22 | 19 | 40 | 42 |
| Kiribati | .. | .. | .. | .. | .. | .. | .. | .. | .. | .. |
| Maldives | .. | .. | .. | .. | .. | .. | .. | .. | .. | .. |
| Solomon Islands | 24 | 18 | 6 | 15 | 4 | 5 | 31 | 29 | 36 | 34 |
| Tonga | 31 | 28 | 6 | 10 | 12 | 6 | 16 | 22 | 36 | 35 |
| Vanuatu | 28 | .. | 7 | .. | 5 | .. | 21 | .. | 40 | .. |
| Western Samoa | 33 | 22 | 4 | 17 | 12 | 4 | 14 | 23 | 37 | 35 |
| ***Other*** | | | | | | | | | | |
| Hong Kong | 25 | 6 | 3 | 2 | 13 | 5 | 13 | 26 | 46 | 60 |
| Japan | 22 | 14 | 20 | 25 | 38 | 16 | 9 | 16 | 11 | 30 |
| Singapore | 23 | 5 | 13 | 16 | 19 | 5 | 14 | 42 | 30 | 32 |
| **MEMORANDUM ITEMS** | | | | | | | | | | |
| United States | 19 | 6 | 10 | 13 | 20 | 5 | 14 | 40 | 36 | 36 |
| European Community | 22 w | 10 w | 11 w | 9 w | 20 w | 8 w | 17 w | 33 w | 30 w | 41 w |
| India | 22 | 7 | 5 | 15 | 14 | 11 | 37 | 31 | 22 | 36 |
| Bangladesh | .. | 30 | .. | 14 | .. | 6 | .. | 17 | .. | 33 |
| Nigeria | 9 | 16 | 6 | 1 | 3 | 4 | 34 | 38 | 48 | 42 |
| Tanzania | 7 | 20 | 9 | 19 | 2 | 4 | 40 | 24 | 42 | 35 |
| Turkey | 6 | 7 | 10 | 21 | 10 | 11 | 37 | 31 | 37 | 30 |
| Hungary | 12 | 7 | 11 | 14 | 22 | 8 | 27 | 35 | 28 | 36 |
| Poland | 14 | 12 | 18 | 13 | 11 | 11 | 27 | 33 | 24 | 32 |
| Egypt, Arab Rep. | 26 | 31 | 7 | 2 | 12 | 10 | 23 | 23 | 31 | 34 |
| Argentina | 6 | 4 | 10 | 9 | 21 | 11 | 25 | 33 | 38 | 44 |
| Brazil | 20 | 9 | 21 | 23 | 9 | 11 | 22 | 27 | 28 | 30 |
| Chile | 20 | 4 | 6 | 12 | 10 | 4 | 35 | 44 | 30 | 36 |
| Mexico | 5 | 16 | 2 | 4 | 10 | 7 | 50 | 36 | 33 | 37 |

# Table 14. Structure of Merchandise Exports

| | Percentage share of merchandise exports | | | | | | | | | |
|---|---|---|---|---|---|---|---|---|---|---|
| | Fuels, minerals, and metals | | Other primary commodities | | Machinery and transport equipment | | Other manufactures | | Textiles and clothing[a] | |
| Country or group | 1965 | 1990 | 1965 | 1990 | 1965 | 1990 | 1965 | 1990 | 1965 | 1990 |
| **GROUP AVERAGES** | | | | | | | | | | |
| Low-income economies | 20 w | 27 w | 49 w | 20 w | 4 w | 9 w | 26 w | 44 w | 16 w | 21 w |
| Middle-income economies | 38 w | 33 w | 39 w | 21 w | 11 w | 17 w | 14 w | 31 w | 3 w | 9 w |
| Low-and middle-income econ. | 34 w | 31 w | 42 w | 21 w | 9 w | 15 w | 17 w | 34 w | 6 w | 12 w |
| Sub-Saharan Africa | 31 w | 64 w | 62 w | 28 w | 0 w | 1 w | 6 w | 7 w | 0 w | 1 w |
| **East Asia & Pacific** | **19 w** | **13 w** | **47 w** | **18 w** | **7 w** | **22 w** | **27 w** | **47 w** | **13 w** | **19 w** |
| South Asia | 6 w | 6 w | 57 w | 25 w | 1 w | 5 w | 36 w | 65 w | 29 w | 33 w |
| Europe | 10 w | 9 w | 21 w | 16 w | 33 w | 26 w | 32 w | 47 w | 8 w | 16 w |
| Middle East & North Africa | 74 w | 75 w | 24 w | 12 w | 0 w | 1 w | 4 w | 16 w | 3 w | 5 w |
| Latin America & Caribbean | 45 w | 38 w | 48 w | 29 w | 1 w | 11 w | 6 w | 21 w | 1 w | 3 w |
| **EAST ASIA AND PACIFIC** | | | | | | | | | | |
| ***Asian tigers*** | | | | | | | | | | |
| Korea, Rep. | 15 | 2 | 25 | 5 | 3 | 37 | 56 | 57 | 27 | 22 |
| Malaysia | 34 | 19 | 60 | 37 | 2 | 27 | 4 | 17 | 0 | 5 |
| Thailand | 11 | 2 | 86 | 34 | 0 | 20 | 3 | 44 | 0 | 16 |
| ***Socialist economies in transition*** | | | | | | | | | | |
| Cambodia | 0 | .. | 99 | .. | 0 | .. | 0 | .. | 0 | .. |
| China | 11 | 10 | 19 | 16 | 15 | 17 | 55 | 56 | 29 | 27 |
| Lao P.D.R. | 62 | .. | 32 | .. | 0 | .. | 6 | .. | 0 | .. |
| Mongolia | .. | .. | .. | .. | .. | .. | .. | .. | .. | .. |
| Myanmar | 5 | 4 | 94 | 93 | 0 | .. | 0 | 3 | 0 | 0 |
| Viet Nam | .. | .. | .. | .. | .. | .. | .. | .. | .. | .. |
| ***Large island economies*** | | | | | | | | | | |
| Indonesia | 43 | 48 | 53 | 16 | 3 | 1 | 1 | 34 | 0 | 11 |
| Papua New Guinea | 0 | 61 | 90 | 34 | .. | 4 | 10 | 1 | .. | 0 |
| Philippines | 11 | 12 | 84 | 26 | 0 | 10 | 6 | 52 | 1 | 7 |

| | | | | | | | | | | |
|---|---|---|---|---|---|---|---|---|---|---|
| ***Pacific island economies*** | | | | | | | | | | |
| Fiji | 1 | 0 | 98 | 90 | 0 | 0 | 0 | 10 | .. | 3 |
| Kiribati | .. | 2 | .. | 98 | .. | .. | .. | .. | .. | .. |
| Maldives | .. | .. | .. | .. | .. | .. | .. | .. | .. | .. |
| Solomon Islands | 2 | .. | 95 | 96 * | .. | .. | 3 | 4 * | .. | .. |
| Tonga | .. | .. | 100 * | 73 * | .. | 2 * | .. | 25 * | .. | 8 * |
| Vanuatu | 26 | .. | 74 | .. | 0 | .. | 0 | .. | .. | .. |
| Western Samoa | .. | 0 | 89 * | 98 | .. | 0 | 11 * | 2 | 0 * | 0 |
| ***Other*** | | | | | | | | | | |
| Hong Kong | 1 | 1 | 5 | 3 | 7 | 23 | 87 | 73 | 52 | 39 |
| Japan | 2 | 1 | 7 | 1 | 31 | 66 | 60 | 32 | 17 | 2 |
| Singapore | 21 | 19 | 44 | 8 | 10 | 48 | 24 | 25 | 6 | 5 |
| **MEMORANDUM ITEMS** | | | | | | | | | | |
| United States | 8 | 6 | 27 | 16 | 37 | 47 | 28 | 31 | 3 | 2 |
| European Community | 8 w | 6 w | 16 w | 12 w | 33 w | 38 w | 43 w | 43 w | 8 w | 6 w |
| India | 10 | 8 | 41 | 19 | 1 | 7 | 47 | 66 | 36 | 23 |
| Bangladesh | .. | 1 | .. | 25 | .. | 1 | .. | 72 | .. | 60 |
| Nigeria | 32 | 97 | 65 | 2 | .. | 0 | 2 | 1 | 0 | 0 |
| Tanzania | 1 | 5 | 86 | 84 | 0 | 1 | 13 | 10 | 0 | 3 |
| Turkey | 9 | 7 | 89 | 25 | 0 | 7 | 2 | 61 | 1 | 37 |
| Hungary | 5 | 9 | 25 | 26 | 32 | 26 | 37 | 40 | 9 | 6 |
| Poland | 20 | 18 | 9 | 15 | 36 | 34 | 25 | 34 | 6 | 5 |
| Egypt, Arab Rep. | 8 | 41 | 71 | 20 | 0 | 0 | 20 | 39 | 15 | 27 |
| Argentina | 1 | 6 | 93 | 59 | 1 | 7 | 5 | 29 | 0 | 3 |
| Brazil | 9 | 16 | 83 | 31 | 2 | 18 | 7 | 35 | 1 | 3 |
| Chile | 89 | 57 | 7 | 33 | 1 | 1 | 4 | 9 | 0 | 1 |
| Mexico | 22 | 43 | 62 | 13 | 1 | 25 | 15 | 19 | 3 | 2 |

a. This category (textiles, yarns, fabrics, and clothing) is a subgroup of Other manufactures.

# Table 15. OECD Imports of Manufactured Goods: Origin and Composition

| Country or group | Value of imports of manufactures, by origin (millions of dollars)[a] | | Composition of 1990 imports of manufactures (percent) | | | | |
|---|---|---|---|---|---|---|---|
| | 1970 | 1990 | Textiles and clothing | Chemicals | Electrical machinery and electronics | Transport equipment | Others |
| **GROUP AVERAGES** | | | | | | | |
| Low-income economies | 1259 t | 59379 t | 40.4 w | 4.9 w | 6.8 w | 2.7 w | 45.2 w |
| Middle-income economies | 5006 t | 175503 t | 25 w | 7.1 w | 16.8 w | 7.1 w | 44 w |
| Low-and middle-income econ. | 6266 t | 234882 t | 28.9 w | 6.5 w | 14.3 w | 6 w | 44.3 w |
| Sub-Saharan Africa | 193 t | 5237 t | 17.2 w | 7.9 w | 0.6 w | 21.8 w | 52.6 w |
| **East Asia & Pacific** | **1077 t** | **108021 t** | **28.8 w** | **3.5 w** | **18.7 w** | **2.6 w** | **46.4 w** |
| South Asia | 755 t | 14676 t | 58 w | 3 w | 0.5 w | 0.7 w | 37.8 w |
| Europe | 2316 t | 47712 t | 37.6 w | 8.7 w | 8.1 w | 6.5 w | 39.1 w |
| Middle East & North Africa | 315 t | 10103 t | 40 w | 19.6 w | 4.7 w | 5.1 w | 30.5 w |
| Latin America & Caribbean | 1285 t | 45896 t | 11.1 w | 8.8 w | 19.3 w | 14 w | 46.8 w |
| **EAST ASIA AND PACIFIC** | | | | | | | |
| ***Asian tigers*** | | | | | | | |
| Korea, Rep. | 524 | 40773 | 24.1 | 2.9 | 19.7 | 5.5 | 47.8 |
| Malaysia | 39 | 9703 | 15.1 | 2.9 | 52.7 | 1.2 | 28.1 |
| Thailand | 32 | 10515 | 22 | 1.5 | 15.7 | 0.9 | 59.9 |
| ***Socialist economies in transition*** | | | | | | | |
| Cambodia | 1 | 2 | 40.8 | 0 | 4.5 | 0.1 | 54.7 |
| China | 243 | 34068 | 36.4 | 5.7 | 11.2 | 0.6 | 46.1 |
| Lao P.D.R. | 0 | 7 | 86.3 | 0 | 0.6 | 0 | 13.2 |
| Mongolia | 0 | 4 | 63.5 | 13.7 | 0.5 | 0 | 22.3 |
| Myanmar | 4 | 43 | 25.2 | 3.2 | 0.2 | 3.3 | 68.1 |
| Viet Nam | 0 | 78 | 76.7 | 3.3 | 0.4 | 0.4 | 19.2 |
| ***Large island economies*** | | | | | | | |
| Indonesia | 15 | 5827 | 35.5 | 2.3 | 1.8 | 0.5 | 60 |
| Papua New Guinea | 4 | 28 | 5.2 | 1.1 | 0.9 | 14.4 | 78.4 |
| Philippines | 108 | 5035 | 35.5 | 2.3 | 28.9 | 0.7 | 32.6 |

| | | | | | | | |
|---|---|---|---|---|---|---|---|
| ***Pacific island economies*** | | | | | | | |
| Fiji | 1 | 89 | 68.6 | 0.4 | 0.5 | 0.1 | 30.4 |
| Kiribati | 0 | 1 | 12 | 1.4 | 6.5 | 0 | 80 |
| Maldives | 0 | 22 | 94 | 0 | 0.8 | 1.1 | 4.1 |
| Solomon Islands | 0 | 7 | 0.4 | 0 | 1 | 0.5 | 98.1 |
| Tonga | 0 | 3 | 47.4 | 0 | 6.1 | 2.4 | 44.1 |
| Vanuatu | 0 | 4 | 11.7 | 0 | 9.1 | 2.5 | 76.7 |
| Western Samoa | 0 | 1 | 34.6 | 3.7 | 5.6 | 3.9 | 52.2 |
| ***Other*** | | | | | | | |
| Hong Kong | 1861 | 24331 | 41.8 | 0.7 | 13.5 | 0.6 | 43.4 |
| Japan | 8851 | 177815 | 1.2 | 3.4 | 19.4 | 29.8 | 46.2 |
| Singapore | 112 | 19504 | 5.4 | 5.6 | 30.3 | 2 | 56.8 |
| **MEMORANDUM ITEMS** | | | | | | | |
| United States | 21215 | 206284 | 2 | 11.8 | 13 | 21.1 | 52.1 |
| European Community | 67309 t | 870227 t | 8.1 w | 15.4 w | 8.9 w | 17.3 w | 50.3 w |
| India | 534 | 9182 | 44.4 | 4.5 | 0.6 | 1 | 49.4 |
| Bangladesh | 0 | 1212 | 86.9 | 0 | 0.2 | 0 | 12.9 |
| Nigeria | 13 | 269 | 5.6 | 15.5 | 1.6 | 1.3 | 76.1 |
| Tanzania | 9 | 47 | 59.9 | 1.6 | 0.6 | 2.4 | 35.5 |
| Turkey | 47 | 6709 | 69.7 | 3.7 | 4.7 | 1.8 | 20.1 |
| Hungary | 210 | 3433 | 22.9 | 17.8 | 10.4 | 3.5 | 45.3 |
| Poland | 287 | 4553 | 20.5 | 17.8 | 7.2 | 5.1 | 49.4 |
| Egypt, Arab Rep. | 33 | 799 | 52.5 | 4.5 | 1.3 | 17.5 | 24.2 |
| Argentina | 104 | 1715 | 10.3 | 18.4 | 1 | 4 | 66.3 |
| Brazil | 197 | 11001 | 7.1 | 9.7 | 5.1 | 13.4 | 64.7 |
| Chile | 15 | 611 | 10.6 | 28.7 | 0.5 | 0.8 | 59.3 |
| Mexico | 508 | 23704 | 4.8 | 4.5 | 33.5 | 17.4 | 39.7 |

a. Trade data are based on the UN Comtrade data base, Revision 1 SITC for 1970 and Revision 2 SITC for 1990.

# Table 16. Balance of Payments and Reserves

| Country or group | Current account balance (millions of dollars): After official transfers 1970 | After official transfers 1990 | Before official transfers 1970 | Before official transfers 1990 | Net workers' remittances (millions of dollars) 1970 | 1990 | Net direct private investment (millions of dollars) 1970 | 1990 | Gross international reserves (millions of dollars) 1970 | 1990 |
|---|---|---|---|---|---|---|---|---|---|---|
| **GROUP AVERAGES** | | | | | | | | | | |
| Low-income economies | | | | | | | | | 3799 t | 63863 t |
| Middle-income economies | | | | | | | | | 16301 t | 194139 t |
| Low-and middle-income econ. | | | | | | | | | 20100 t | 258002 t |
| Sub-Saharan Africa | | | | | | | | | 2028 t | 12684 t |
| **East Asia & Pacific** | | | | | | | | | **2885 t** | **85907 t** |
| South Asia | | | | | | | | | 1453 t | 8665 t |
| Europe | | | | | | | | | 2624 t | 49920 t |
| Middle East & North Africa | | | | | | | | | 4526 t | 39533 t |
| Latin America & Caribbean | | | | | | | | | 5527 t | 58710 t |
| **EAST ASIA AND PACIFIC** | | | | | | | | | | |
| ***Asian tigers*** | | | | | | | | | | |
| Korea, Rep. | -623 | -2172 | -706 | -2181 | .. | 0 * | 66 | -105 | 610 | 14916 |
| Malaysia | 8 | -1672 | 2 | -1733 | .. | .. | 94 | 2902 | 667 | 10659 |
| Thailand | -250 | -7053 | -296 | -7235 | .. | 74 | 43 | 2236 | 911 | 14258 |
| ***Socialist economies in transition*** | | | | | | | | | | |
| Cambodia | .. | .. | .. | .. | .. | .. | .. | .. | .. | .. |
| China | -81 | 12000 | -81 | 11935 | 0 | 108 | .. | 2613 | .. | 34476 |
| Lao P.D.R. | .. | -106 | .. | -148 | .. | .. | .. | .. | 6 | 61 |
| Mongolia | .. | -640 | .. | -647 | .. | 0 | .. | .. | .. | .. |
| Myanmar | -63 | -163 * | -81 | -204 * | .. | 0 * | .. | 154 * | 98 | 410 |
| Viet Nam | .. | -213 | .. | -323 | .. | .. | .. | .. | 243 | .. |
| ***Large island economies*** | | | | | | | | | | |
| Indonesia | -310 | -2369 | -376 | -2430 | .. | 153 | 83 | 964 | 160 | 8657 |
| Papua New Guinea | -89 | -352 | -239 | -566 | .. | 51 | .. | 231 | .. | 427 |
| Philippines | -48 | -2695 | -138 | -3052 | .. | 262 | -29 | 530 | 255 | 2036 |

| | | | | | | | | | | |
|---|---|---|---|---|---|---|---|---|---|---|
| ***Pacific island economies*** | | | | | | | | | | |
| Fiji | -14 | 7 | -18 | -18 | .. | .. | 6 | 30 | 27 | 261 |
| Kiribati | .. | .. | .. | .. | .. | .. | .. | .. | .. | .. |
| Maldives | .. | 2 | .. | -10 | .. | -10 | .. | 3 | .. | 24 |
| Solomon Islands | .. | -26 | .. | -59 | .. | -5 | .. | 13 | .. | 18 |
| Tonga | -1 * | 8 | -1 * | -2 | 1 * | 15 | .. | 0 | .. | 31 |
| Vanuatu | .. | 8 | .. | -21 | .. | 2 | .. | 13 | .. | 38 |
| Western Samoa | -5 | 2 | -5 | -12 | 3 | 43 | .. | .. | 5 | 69 |
| ***Other*** | | | | | | | | | | |
| Hong Kong | 225 | .. | 225 | .. | .. | .. | .. | .. | .. | .. |
| Japan | 1990 | 35870 | 2170 | 40380 | .. | .. | -260 | -46290 | 4876 | 87828 |
| Singapore | -572 | 2350 | -585 | 2445 | .. | .. | 93 | 4489 | 1012 | 27748 |
| **MEMORANDUM ITEMS** | | | | | | | | | | |
| United States | 2330 | -92160 | 4680 | -71710 | -650 | -1100 | -6130 | 3750 | 15237 | 173094 |
| European Community | | | | | | | | | 35826 t | 438106 t |
| India | -385 | -9304 | -591 | -9828 | 80 | 1947 | 0 | 253 | 1023 | 5637 |
| Bangladesh | -114 | -775 | -234 | -1541 | 0 | 761 | .. | 0 | .. | 660 |
| Nigeria | -368 | 5126 | -412 | 5027 | .. | -14 | 205 | 588 | 223 | 4129 |
| Tanzania | -36 | -426 | -37 | -955 | .. | 0 * | .. | 5 | 65 | 193 |
| Turkey | -44 | -2616 | -57 | -3778 | 273 | 3246 | 58 | 681 | 440 | 7626 |
| Hungary | -25 | 230 | -25 | 230 | .. | 0 * | .. | 337 | .. | 1186 |
| Poland | .. | 3067 | .. | 2762 | .. | 0 | .. | 89 | .. | 4674 |
| Egypt, Arab Rep. | -148 | -1425 | -452 | -2535 | 29 | 3744 | .. | 136 | 165 | 3620 |
| Argentina | -163 | 1789 | -160 | 1789 | .. | 0 * | 11 | 2036 | 682 | 6222 |
| Brazil | -837 | -2983 | -861 | -2983 | .. | .. | 407 | 510 | 1190 | 9200 |
| Chile | -91 | -790 | -95 | -935 | .. | .. | -79 | 587 | 392 | 6784 |
| Mexico | -1068 | -5255 | -1098 | -6521 | .. | 2020 | 323 | 2632 | 756 | 10217 |

# Table 17. Official Development Assistance: Receipts

| | Net disbursements of ODA from all sources | | | | | | | | |
|---|---|---|---|---|---|---|---|---|---|
| | Millions of dollars | | | | | | | Per capita (dollars) | As percentage of GNP |
| *Country or group* | *1984* | *1985* | *1986* | *1987* | *1988* | *1989* | *1990* | *1990* | *1990* |
| **GROUP AVERAGES** | | | | | | | | | |
| Low-income economies | 14476 t | 15896 t | 18781 t | 20555 t | 23722 t | 23862 t | 29353 t | 9.6 w | 2.8 w |
| Middle-income economies | 9557 t | 9756 t | 11438 t | 12607 t | 11847 t | 12446 t | 17882 t | 18.7 w | 0.7 w |
| Low-and middle-income econ. | 24033 t | 25653 t | 30219 t | 33162 t | 35570 t | 36307 t | 47235 t | 11.8 w | 1.4 w |
| Sub-Saharan Africa | 7941 t | 9006 t | 11093 t | 12500 t | 14077 t | 14505 t | 16810 t | 33.9 w | 9.6 w |
| **East Asia & Pacific** | **3553 t** | **3577 t** | **4529 t** | **5548 t** | **6405 t** | **7053 t** | **7771 t** | **4.9 w** | **0.8 w** |
| South Asia | 4585 t | 4655 t | 5888 t | 5630 t | 6615 t | 6118 t | 6174 t | 5.4 w | 1.6 w |
| Europe | 376 t | 348 t | 543 t | 522 t | 461 t | 285 t | 1420 t | 14.1 w | 0.4 w |
| Middle East & North Africa | 4506 t | 4668 t | 4405 t | 4745 t | 3743 t | 3622 t | 9680 t | 37.8 w | 3.4 w |
| Latin America & Caribbean | 3072 t | 3400 t | 3761 t | 4217 t | 4269 t | 4724 t | 5380 t | 12.3 w | 0.4 w |
| **EAST ASIA AND PACIFIC** | | | | | | | | | |
| ***Asian tigers*** | | | | | | | | | |
| Korea, Rep. | -37 | -9 | -18 | 11 | 10 | 52 | 52 | 1.2 | 0 |
| Malaysia | 327 | 229 | 192 | 363 | 104 | 140 | 469 | 26.3 | 1.1 |
| Thailand | 475 | 481 | 496 | 504 | 563 | 739 | 805 | 14.4 | 1 |
| ***Socialist economies in transition*** | | | | | | | | | |
| China | 798 | 940 | 1134 | 1462 | 1989 | 2153 | 2076 | 1.8 | 0.6 |
| Cambodia | 17 | 13 | 13 | 14 | 18 | 31 | 42 | 4.9 | .. |
| Lao P.D.R. | 34 | 37 | 48 | 58 | 77 | 140 | 152 | 36.6 | 17.5 |
| Mongolia | .. | .. | .. | .. | .. | .. | .. | .. | .. |
| Myanmar | 275 | 356 | 416 | 367 | 451 | 184 | 170 | 4.1 | 0.8 |
| Viet Nam | 109 | 114 | 147 | 111 | 148 | 129 | 190 | 2.9 | 2.1 |
| ***Large island economies*** | | | | | | | | | |
| Indonesia | 673 | 603 | 711 | 1246 | 1632 | 1839 | 1724 | 9.7 | 1.6 |
| Papua New Guinea | 322 | 259 | 263 | 322 | 380 | 339 | 376 | 96.1 | 11.4 |
| Philippines | 397 | 486 | 956 | 770 | 854 | 844 | 1277 | 20.8 | 2.9 |

| | | | | | | | | | |
|---|---|---|---|---|---|---|---|---|---|
| ***Pacific island economies*** | | | | | | | | | |
| Fiji | 31 | 32 | 43 | 36 | 54 | 43 | 49 | 66.4 | 3.6 |
| Kiribati | 12 | 12 | 14 | 18 | 16 | 17 | 20 | 291.4 | .. |
| Maldives | 6 | 9 | 16 | 19 | 27 | 28 | 22 | 103.3 | 21.9 |
| Solomon Islands | 19 | 21 | 30 | 57 | 58 | 49 | 44 | 140.2 | 26.1 |
| Tonga | 16 | 13 | 15 | 21 | 19 | 25 | 31 | 312.1 | 32.6 |
| Vanuatu | 24 | 22 | 24 | 51 | 39 | 40 | 49 | 323.2 | .. |
| Western Samoa | 20 | 19 | 23 | 35 | 31 | 31 | 51 | 307.3 | 44.1 |
| ***Other*** | | | | | | | | | |
| Hong Kong | 14 | 20 | 18 | 19 | 22 | 40 | 37 | 6.4 | 0.1 |
| Japan | .. | .. | .. | .. | .. | .. | .. | .. | .. |
| Singapore | 41 | 24 | 29 | 23 | 22 | 95 | -3 | -1 | 0 |
| **MEMORANDUM ITEMS** | | | | | | | | | |
| United States | .. | .. | .. | .. | .. | .. | .. | .. | .. |
| European Community | 109 t | 111 t | 158 t | 99 t | 137 t | 108 t | 102 t | 5 w | 0.1 w |
| India | 1673 | 1592 | 2120 | 1839 | 2097 | 1895 | 1586 | 1.9 | 0.6 |
| Bangladesh | 1200 | 1152 | 1455 | 1635 | 1592 | 1800 | 2103 | 19.7 | 9.2 |
| Nigeria | 33 | 32 | 59 | 69 | 120 | 346 | 234 | 2 | 0.7 |
| Tanzania | 558 | 487 | 681 | 882 | 982 | 920 | 1155 | 47.1 | 48.2 |
| Turkey | 242 | 179 | 339 | 376 | 267 | 140 | 1264 | 22.5 | 1.2 |
| Hungary | .. | .. | .. | .. | .. | .. | .. | .. | .. |
| Poland | .. | .. | .. | .. | .. | .. | .. | .. | .. |
| Egypt, Arab Rep. | 1794 | 1791 | 1716 | 1773 | 1537 | 1568 | 5604 | 107.6 | 15.9 |
| Argentina | 49 | 39 | 88 | 99 | 152 | 211 | 172 | 5.3 | 0.2 |
| Brazil | 161 | 123 | 178 | 289 | 210 | 206 | 164 | 1.1 | 0 |
| Chile | 2 | 40 | -5 | 21 | 44 | 61 | 94 | 7.1 | 0.3 |
| Mexico | 83 | 144 | 252 | 155 | 173 | 86 | 140 | 1.6 | 0.1 |

## Table 18. Total External Debt

| Country or group | Long-term debt (millions of dollars): Public and publicly guaranteed 1970 | 1990 | Private nonguaranteed 1970 | 1990 | Use of IMF credit (millions of dollars) 1970 | 1990 | Short-term debt (millions of dollars) 1970 | 1990 | Total external debt (millions of dollars) 1970 | 1990 |
|---|---|---|---|---|---|---|---|---|---|---|
| **GROUP AVERAGES** | | | | | | | | | | |
| Low-income economies | | | | | | | | | | |
| Middle-income economies | | | | | | | | | | |
| Low-and middle-income econ. | | | | | | | | | | |
| Sub-Saharan Africa | | | | | | | | | | |
| **East Asia & Pacific** | | | | | | | | | | |
| South Asia | | | | | | | | | | |
| Europe | | | | | | | | | | |
| Middle East & North Africa | | | | | | | | | | |
| Latin America & Caribbean | | | | | | | | | | |
| **EAST ASIA AND PACIFIC** | | | | | | | | | | |
| ***Asian tigers*** | | | | | | | | | | |
| Korea, Rep. | 1816 | 17814 | 175 | 5400 | 0 | 0 | 0 | 10800 | 1991 | 34014 |
| Malaysia | 390 | 16107 | 50 | 1489 | 0 | 0 | 0 | 1906 | 440 | 19502 |
| Thailand | 324 | 12572 | 402 | 4973 | 0 | 1 | 0 | 8322 | 726 | 25868 |
| ***Socialist economies in transition*** | | | | | | | | | | |
| Cambodia | .. | .. | .. | .. | .. | .. | .. | .. | .. | .. |
| China | 0 | 45319 | 0 | 0 | 0 | 469 | 0 | 6766 | 0 | 52555 |
| Lao P.D.R. | 8 | 1053 | 0 | 0 | 0 | 8 | 0 | 2 | 8 | 1063 |
| Mongolia | .. | .. | .. | .. | .. | .. | .. | .. | .. | .. |
| Myanmar | 106 | 4447 | 0 | 0 | 17 | 0 | 0 | 229 | 123 | 4675 |
| Viet Nam | .. | .. | .. | .. | .. | .. | .. | .. | .. | .. |
| ***Large island economies*** | | | | | | | | | | |
| Indonesia | 2497 | 44974 | 461 | 9405 | 139 | 494 | 0 | 13035 | 3096 | 67908 |
| Papua New Guinea | 36 | 1509 | 173 | 965 | 0 | 61 | 0 | 72 | 209 | 2606 |
| Philippines | 625 | 24108 | 919 | 1006 | 69 | 912 | 0 | 4431 | 1613 | 30456 |

| | | | | | | | | | | |
|---|---|---|---|---|---|---|---|---|---|---|
| ***Pacific island economies*** | | | | | | | | | | |
| Fiji | 12 | 292 | 0 | 95 | 0 | 0 | 0 | 12 | 12 | 399 |
| Kiribati | .. | .. | .. | .. | .. | .. | .. | .. | .. | .. |
| Maldives | 0 | 64 | 0 | 0 | 0 | 0 | 0 | 14 | 0 | 78 |
| Solomon Islands | 0 | 105 | 0 | 0 | 0 | 1 | 0 | 17 | 0 | 123 |
| Tonga | 0 | 49 | 0 | 0 | 0 | 0 | 0 | 9 | 0 | 58 |
| Vanuatu | 1 | 31 | 0 | 0 | 0 | 0 | 0 | 10 | 1 | 40 |
| Western Samoa | 3 | 92 | 0 | 0 | 0 | 1 | 0 | 0 | 3 | 93 |
| ***Other*** | | | | | | | | | | |
| Hong Kong | .. | .. | .. | .. | .. | .. | .. | .. | .. | .. |
| Japan | .. | .. | .. | .. | .. | .. | .. | .. | .. | .. |
| Singapore | .. | .. | .. | .. | .. | .. | .. | .. | .. | .. |
| **MEMORANDUM ITEMS** | | | | | | | | | | |
| United States | .. | .. | .. | .. | .. | .. | .. | .. | .. | .. |
| European Community | | | | | | | | | | |
| India | 7838 | 61097 | 100 | 1488 | 0 | 2623 | 0 | 4908 | 7938 | 70115 |
| Bangladesh | 15 | 11464 | 0 | 0 | 0 | 626 | 0 | 156 | 15 | 12245 |
| Nigeria | 452 | 33709 | 115 | 391 | 0 | 0 | 0 | 1968 | 567 | 36068 |
| Tanzania | 180 | 5294 | 15 | 12 | 0 | 140 | 0 | 420 | 195 | 5866 |
| Turkey | 1846 | 38595 | 42 | 1054 | 74 | 0 | 0 | 9500 | 1962 | 49149 |
| Hungary | 0 | 18046 | 0 | 0 | 0 | 330 | 0 | 2941 | 0 | 21316 |
| Poland | 24 | 39282 | 0 | 0 | 0 | 509 | 0 | 9595 | 24 | 49386 |
| Egypt, Arab Rep. | 1517 | 34242 | 0 | 1000 | 49 | 125 | 0 | 4518 | 1567 | 39885 |
| Argentina | 1880 | 46146 | 3291 | 1800 | 0 | 3083 | 0 | 10115 | 5171 | 61144 |
| Brazil | 3426 | 82098 | 1706 | 7771 | 0 | 1821 | 0 | 24483 | 5132 | 116173 |
| Chile | 2067 | 10339 | 501 | 4263 | 2 | 1157 | 0 | 3356 | 2570 | 19114 |
| Mexico | 3196 | 76204 | 2770 | 4409 | 0 | 6551 | 0 | 9645 | 5966 | 96810 |

# Table 19. Flow of Public and Private External Capital

| | Disbursements (millions of dollars) | | | | Repayment of principal (millions of dollars) | | | | Interest payments on long-term public and publicly guaranteed (millions of dollars) | |
|---|---|---|---|---|---|---|---|---|---|---|
| | Long-term public and publicly guaranteed | | Private nonguaranteed | | Long-term public and publicly guaranteed | | Private nonguaranteed | | | |
| *Country or group* | *1970* | *1990* | *1970* | *1990* | *1970* | *1990* | *1970* | *1990* | *1970* | *1990* |
| **GROUP AVERAGES** | | | | | | | | | | |
| Low-income economies | | | | | | | | | | |
| Middle-income economies | | | | | | | | | | |
| Low-and middle-income econ. | | | | | | | | | | |
| Sub-Saharan Africa | | | | | | | | | | |
| **East Asia & Pacific** | | | | | | | | | | |
| South Asia | | | | | | | | | | |
| Europe | | | | | | | | | | |
| Middle East & North Africa | | | | | | | | | | |
| Latin America & Caribbean | | | | | | | | | | |
| **EAST ASIA AND PACIFIC** | | | | | | | | | | |
| ***Asian tigers*** | | | | | | | | | | |
| Korea, Rep. | 444 | 3198 | 32 | 1529 | 198 | 3539 | 7 | 2090 | 71 | 1267 |
| Malaysia | 45 | 1779 | 12 | 685 | 47 | 2220 | 9 | 470 | 22 | 1125 |
| Thailand | 51 | 1513 | 169 | 1149 | 23 | 2424 | 107 | 847 | 16 | 877 |
| ***Socialist economies in transition*** | | | | | | | | | | |
| Cambodia | .. | .. | .. | .. | .. | .. | .. | .. | .. | .. |
| China | 0 | 9620 | 0 | 0 | 0 | 3371 | 0 | 0 | 0 | 2534 |
| Lao P.D.R. | 6 | 107 | 0 | 0 | 1 | 8 | 0 | 0 | 0 | 3 |
| Mongolia | .. | .. | .. | .. | .. | .. | .. | .. | .. | .. |
| Myanmar | 22 | 122 | 0 | 0 | 20 | 45 | 0 | 0 | 3 | 13 |
| Viet Nam | .. | .. | .. | .. | .. | .. | .. | .. | .. | .. |
| ***Large island economies*** | | | | | | | | | | |
| Indonesia | 441 | 4615 | 195 | 5533 | 59 | 4140 | 61 | 977 | 25 | 2536 |
| Papua New Guinea | 43 | 275 | 111 | 205 | 0 | 174 | 20 | 199 | 1 | 86 |
| Philippines | 141 | 2155 | 276 | 291 | 74 | 705 | 186 | 47 | 26 | 1471 |

| | | | | | | | | | | |
|---|---|---|---|---|---|---|---|---|---|---|
| ***Pacific island economies*** | | | | | | | | | | |
| Fiji | 2 | 16 | 0 | 14 | 2 | 55 | 0 | 18 | 1 | 24 |
| Kiribati | .. | .. | .. | .. | .. | .. | .. | .. | .. | .. |
| Maldives | 0 | 13 | 0 | 0 | 0 | 6 | 0 | 0 | 0 | 1 |
| Solomon Islands | 0 | 7 | 0 | 0 | 0 | 7 | 0 | 0 | 0 | 3 |
| Tonga | 0 | 1 | 0 | 0 | 0 | 1 | 0 | 0 | 0 | 1 |
| Vanuatu | 0 | 9 | 0 | 0 | 0 | 1 | 0 | 0 | 0 | 1 |
| Western Samoa | 2 | 16 | 0 | 0 | 0 | 3 | 0 | 0 | 0 | 1 |
| ***Other*** | | | | | | | | | | |
| Hong Kong | .. | .. | .. | .. | .. | .. | .. | .. | .. | .. |
| Japan | .. | .. | .. | .. | .. | .. | .. | .. | .. | .. |
| Singapore | .. | .. | .. | .. | .. | .. | .. | .. | .. | .. |
| **MEMORANDUM ITEMS** | | | | | | | | | | |
| United States | .. | .. | .. | .. | .. | .. | .. | .. | .. | .. |
| European Community | | | | | | | | | | |
| India | 883 | 5191 | 25 | 214 | 289 | 2162 | 25 | 318 | 187 | 3275 |
| Bangladesh | 0 | 1121 | 0 | 0 | 0 | 275 | 0 | 0 | 0 | 159 |
| Nigeria | 56 | 727 | 25 | 0 | 38 | 1205 | 30 | 15 | 20 | 1758 |
| Tanzania | 51 | 299 | 8 | 0 | 2 | 53 | 3 | 0 | 3 | 46 |
| Turkey | 331 | 4344 | 1 | 543 | 128 | 3426 | 3 | 283 | 42 | 2763 |
| Hungary | 0 | 2573 | 0 | 0 | 0 | 2233 | 0 | 0 | 0 | 1571 |
| Poland | 30 | 540 | 0 | 0 | 6 | 642 | 0 | 0 | 0 | 206 |
| Egypt, Arab Rep. | 199 | 2192 | 0 | 102 | 227 | 1715 | 0 | 183 | 40 | 1054 |
| Argentina | 482 | 914 | 424 | 0 | 344 | 1664 | 428 | 0 | 121 | 2129 |
| Brazil | 896 | 2686 | 900 | 875 | 256 | 2718 | 200 | 1008 | 135 | 2223 |
| Chile | 408 | 707 | 247 | 1545 | 166 | 474 | 41 | 271 | 78 | 1096 |
| Mexico | 772 | 7901 | 603 | 1484 | 475 | 2615 | 542 | 1046 | 216 | 5365 |

# Table 20. Total External Debt Ratios

| Country or group | Total debt as a percentage of: Exports of goods and services 1980 | Total debt as a percentage of: Exports of goods and services 1990 | Total debt as a percentage of: GNP 1980 | Total debt as a percentage of: GNP 1990 | Total debt service as a percentage of exports of goods and services 1980 | Total debt service as a percentage of exports of goods and services 1990 | Interest payments as a percentage of exports of goods and services 1980 | Interest payments as a percentage of exports of goods and services 1990 |
|---|---|---|---|---|---|---|---|---|
| **GROUP AVERAGES** | | | | | | | | |
| Low-income economies | 105.1 w | 218.5 w | 16.4 w | 41 w | 10.3 w | 20.1 w | 5.1 w | 9.3 w |
| Middle-income economies | 135.2 w | 155.6 w | 31.9 w | 39.9 w | 24.3 w | 19.1 w | 12.5 w | 8.3 w |
| Low-and middle-income econ. | 127 w | 171.3 w | 26.2 w | 40.2 w | 20.5 w | 19.4 w | 10.5 w | 8.5 w |
| Sub-Saharan Africa | 96.8 w | 324.3 w | 28.5 w | 109.4 w | 10.9 w | 19.3 w | 5.7 w | 8.9 w |
| **East Asia & Pacific** | **88.8 w** | **91.1 w** | **16.8 w** | **26.9 w** | **13.5 w** | **14.6 w** | **7.7 w** | **5.8 w** |
| South Asia | 162.9 w | 281.5 w | 17.3 w | 30.7 w | 12.2 w | 25.9 w | 5.2 w | 13.1 w |
| Europe | 90.6 w | 125.7 w | 23.8 w | 41 w | 15.9 w | 16.9 w | 7.1 w | 6.8 w |
| Middle East & N.Africa | 114.9 w | 180.3 w | 31.1 w | 52.6 w | 16.4 w | 24.4 w | 7.4 w | 8.1 w |
| Latin America & Caribbean | 196.8 w | 257.4 w | 35.2 w | 41.6 w | 37.3 w | 25 w | 19.7 w | 13.3 w |
| **EAST ASIA AND PACIFIC** | | | | | | | | |
| ***Asian tigers*** | | | | | | | | |
| Korea, Rep. | 130.6 | 44 | 48.7 | 14.4 | 19.7 | 10.7 | 12.7 | 3.5 |
| Malaysia | 44.6 | 55.9 | 28 | 48 | 6.3 | 11.7 | 4 | 4 |
| Thailand | 96.8 | 82 | 26 | 32.6 | 18.9 | 17.2 | 9.5 | 6 |
| ***Socialist economies in transition*** | | | | | | | | |
| Cambodia | .. | .. | .. | .. | .. | .. | .. | .. |
| China | 21.2 | 77.4 | 1.5 | 14.4 | 4.4 | 10.3 | 1.5 | 4.6 |
| Lao P.D.R. | .. | 1113.5 | .. | 123.3 | .. | 12.1 | .. | 3.2 |
| Mongolia | .. | .. | .. | .. | .. | .. | .. | .. |
| Myanmar | 269.9 | .. | 26 | 21.1 | 25.4 | .. | 9.4 | .. |
| Viet Nam | .. | .. | .. | .. | .. | .. | .. | .. |
| ***Large island economies*** | | | | | | | | |
| Indonesia | 94.2 | 229.4 | 28 | 66.4 | 13.9 | 30.9 | 6.5 | 13.1 |
| Papua New Guinea | 66.1 | 168.6 | 29.2 | 83.9 | 13.8 | 36 | 6.6 | 11.7 |
| Philippines | 212.3 | 229.2 | 53.8 | 69.3 | 26.6 | 21.2 | 18.2 | 13 |

| | | | | | | | | |
|---|---|---|---|---|---|---|---|---|
| ***Pacific island economies*** | | | | | | | | |
| Fiji | 46.8 | 42.8 | 23.7 | 29.6 | 6 | 11.3 | 2.7 | 3.5 |
| Kiribati | .. | .. | .. | .. | .. | .. | .. | .. |
| Maldives | 39.6 | 45.7 | 108.2 | 86.4 | 0.9 | 5 | 0.9 | 1.6 |
| Solomon Islands | 22.8 | 121.1 | 18 | 72.4 | 0.4 | 11.9 | 0.4 | 3.9 |
| Tonga | 109.1 | 103.3 | .. | 59.9 | 0.6 | 4.2 | 0 | 2.8 |
| Vanuatu | .. | 34.5 | 4.3 | 24.8 | .. | 2.1 | .. | 1.2 |
| Western Samoa | 135.5 | 105.9 | .. | 77 | 12.4 | 6.4 | 6.1 | 1.5 |
| ***Other*** | | | | | | | | |
| Hong Kong | .. | .. | .. | .. | .. | .. | .. | .. |
| Japan | .. | .. | .. | .. | .. | .. | .. | .. |
| Singapore | .. | .. | .. | .. | .. | .. | .. | .. |
| **MEMORANDUM ITEMS** | | | | | | | | |
| United States | .. | .. | .. | .. | .. | .. | .. | .. |
| European Community | 99.5 w | 75.4 w | 40.5 w | 36.5 w | 18.3 w | 17.8 w | 10.5 w | 5.3 w |
| India | 136 | 282.4 | 11.9 | 25 | 9.3 | 28.8 | 4.2 | 15.9 |
| Bangladesh | 345.6 | 448.2 | 31.3 | 53.8 | 23.2 | 25.4 | 6.4 | 7.7 |
| Nigeria | 32.2 | 242.7 | 10 | 110.9 | 4.2 | 20.3 | 3.3 | 12.1 |
| Tanzania | 317.8 | 1070.7 | 47.7 | 282 | 19.6 | 25.8 | 10 | 10.9 |
| Turkey | 332.9 | 195 | 34.3 | 46.1 | 28 | 28.2 | 14.9 | 13.3 |
| Hungary | 95.9 | 188.6 | 44.8 | 67.8 | 18.9 | 37.9 | 10.8 | 15.2 |
| Poland | 54.9 | 251.5 | 16.3 | 82 | 17.9 | 4.9 | 5.2 | 1.6 |
| Egypt, Arab Rep. | 227.7 | 300.8 | 97.8 | 126.5 | 14.8 | 25.7 | 9.2 | 11 |
| Argentina | 242.4 | 405.6 | 48.4 | 61.7 | 37.3 | 34.1 | 20.8 | 18.4 |
| Brazil | 304.9 | 326.8 | 31.2 | 25.1 | 63.1 | 20.8 | 33.8 | 8.2 |
| Chile | 192.5 | 181.3 | 45.2 | 73.5 | 43.1 | 25.9 | 19 | 16.8 |
| Mexico | 259.2 | 222 | 30.5 | 42.1 | 49.5 | 27.8 | 27.4 | 16.7 |

# Table 21. Terms of External Public Borrowing

| Country or group | Commitments (millions of dollars) | | Average interest rate (percent) | | Average maturity (years) | | Average grace period (years) | | Public loans with variable interest rates, as a percentage of public debt | |
|---|---|---|---|---|---|---|---|---|---|---|
| | 1970 | 1990 | 1970 | 1990 | 1970 | 1990 | 1970 | 1990 | 1970 | 1990 |
| **GROUP AVERAGES** | | | | | | | | | | |
| Low-income economies | 4823 t | 36364 t | 3.2 w | 5.4 w | 28.5 w | 23.4 w | 8.4 w | 6.5 w | 0.1 w | 19 w |
| Middle-income economies | 7300 t | 56313 t | 6.3 w | 7.8 w | 15.9 w | 14.2 w | 4.1 w | 4.8 w | 2.9 w | 47.6 w |
| Low-and middle-income econ. | 12123 t | 92677 t | 5 w | 6.8 w | 20.9 w | 17.8 w | 5.9 w | 5.4 w | 1.7 w | 37.8 w |
| Sub-Saharan Africa | 1890 t | 9577 t | 3.6 w | 3.9 w | 25.6 w | 26.1 w | 7.8 w | 7 w | 0.9 w | 18.2 w |
| **East Asia & Pacific** | **1689 t** | **25581 t** | **5 w** | **6.8 w** | **23.2 w** | **18.6 w** | **6.4 w** | **5.5 w** | **0.5 w** | **33.1 w** |
| South Asia | 2052 t | 12223 t | 2.7 w | 4.4 w | 32.1 w | 25.8 w | 9.7 w | 7.8 w | 0 w | 12.9 w |
| Europe | 755 t | 14366 t | 4.6 w | 8.7 w | 18.5 w | 11.5 w | 5 w | 4.9 w | 1.5 w | 51.2 w |
| Middle East & N.Africa | 1366 t | 11429 t | 4.3 w | 7.7 w | 17.2 w | 13.4 w | 4.6 w | 3.7 w | 0.6 w | 24.1 w |
| Latin America & Caribbean | 4372 t | 19501 t | 7 w | 8 w | 14.4 w | 15 w | 3.6 w | 4.6 w | 4 w | 55.9 w |
| **EAST ASIA AND PACIFIC** | | | | | | | | | | |
| ***Asian tigers*** | | | | | | | | | | |
| Korea, Rep. | 691 | 2027 | 5.8 | 7.1 | 19 | 13 | 6 | 7 | 1.2 | 22.7 |
| Malaysia | 84 | 2270 | 6.1 | 7.4 | 19 | 14 | 5 | 5 | 0 | 48.8 |
| Thailand | 106 | 1721 | 6.8 | 5.5 | 19 | 21 | 4 | 7 | 0 | 24.5 |
| ***Socialist economies in transition*** | | | | | | | | | | |
| Cambodia | .. | .. | .. | .. | .. | .. | .. | .. | .. | .. |
| China | 0 | 9786 | 0 | 7.6 | 0 | 17 | 0 | 4 | 0 | 36.4 |
| Lao P.D.R. | 12 | 139 | 3 | 0.8 | 28 | 40 | 4 | 15 | 0 | 0 |
| Mongolia | .. | .. | .. | .. | .. | .. | .. | .. | .. | .. |
| Myanmar | 48 | 0 | 4.1 | 0 | 16 | 0 | 5 | 0 | 0 | 0 |
| Viet Nam | .. | .. | .. | .. | .. | .. | .. | .. | .. | .. |
| ***Large island economies*** | | | | | | | | | | |
| Indonesia | 530 | 6071 | 2.6 | 6 | 34 | 22 | 9 | 6 | 0 | 28.4 |
| Papua New Guinea | 91 | 200 | 6.4 | 6.4 | 22 | 15 | 8 | 5 | 0 | 27.1 |
| Philippines | 171 | 3249 | 7.3 | 6 | 11 | 22 | 2 | 7 | 0.8 | 40.2 |

| | | | | | | | | | | |
|---|---|---|---|---|---|---|---|---|---|---|
| ***Pacific island economies*** | | | | | | | | | | |
| Fiji | 4 | 28 | 3.2 | 7.3 | 18 | 24 | 5 | 5 | 0 | 9.3 |
| Kiribati | .. | .. | .. | .. | .. | .. | .. | .. | .. | .. |
| Maldives | 0 | 12 | 0 | 0.8 | 0 | 41 | 0 | 10 | 0 | 0 |
| Solomon Islands | 1 | 0 | 0 | 0 | 29 | 0 | 13 | 0 | 0 | 10.4 |
| Tonga | 0 | 72 | 0 | 1 | 0 | 40 | 0 | 10 | 0 | 0 |
| Vanuatu | 0 | 0 | 0 | 0 | 0 | 0 | 0 | 0 | 0 | 2.6 |
| Western Samoa | 1 | 17 | 5 | 0.9 | 20 | 38 | 6 | 10 | 0 | 0 |
| ***Other*** | | | | | | | | | | |
| Hong Kong | .. | .. | .. | .. | .. | .. | .. | .. | .. | .. |
| Japan | .. | .. | .. | .. | .. | .. | .. | .. | .. | .. |
| Singapore | .. | .. | .. | .. | .. | .. | .. | .. | .. | .. |
| **MEMORANDUM ITEMS** | | | | | | | | | | |
| United States | .. | .. | .. | .. | .. | .. | .. | .. | .. | .. |
| European Community | 59 t | 3573 t | 4.3 w | 8.3 w | 16.9 w | 16.3 w | 3.9 w | 5.1 w | 0 w | 29 w |
| India | 954 | 6896 | 2.5 | 4.8 | 34 | 25 | 8 | 8 | 0 | 17.5 |
| Bangladesh | 0 | 1325 | 0 | 2 | 0 | 34 | 0 | 9 | 0 | 0 |
| Nigeria | 65 | 2017 | 6 | 6.7 | 14 | 19 | 4 | 4 | 2.7 | 34.5 |
| Tanzania | 271 | 603 | 1 | 0.8 | 40 | 37 | 11 | 10 | 0 | 4.5 |
| Turkey | 489 | 3654 | 3.6 | 8.9 | 19 | 10 | 5 | 5 | 0.9 | 32.4 |
| Hungary | 0 | 3285 | 0 | 8.9 | 0 | 8 | 0 | 5 | 0 | 59.5 |
| Poland | 0 | 1474 | 0 | 8.3 | 0 | 14 | 0 | 5 | 0 | 67 |
| Egypt, Arab Rep. | 528 | 800 | 4.1 | 5.3 | 17 | 27 | 5 | 8 | 0 | 11.3 |
| Argentina | 494 | 459 | 7.3 | 8.5 | 12 | 9 | 3 | 2 | 0 | 80.3 |
| Brazil | 1439 | 1862 | 7 | 8.5 | 14 | 12 | 3 | 5 | 11.8 | 69.2 |
| Chile | 361 | 1041 | 6.8 | 7.8 | 12 | 17 | 3 | 4 | 0 | 65.6 |
| Mexico | 858 | 8004 | 7.9 | 8.6 | 12 | 13 | 3 | 4 | 5.7 | 46.3 |

## Table 22. Population Growth and Projections

| Country or group | Average annual growth of population (percent) | | | Population (millions) | | | Hypothetical size of stationary population (thousands) | Age structure of population (percent) | | |
|---|---|---|---|---|---|---|---|---|---|---|
| | | | | | | | | 0–14 years | | 15–64 years |
| | 1965–80 | 1980–90 | 1990–2000[a] | 1990 | 2000[a] | 2025[a] | | 1990 | 2025[a] | 1990 |
| **GROUP AVERAGES** | | | | | | | | | | |
| Low-income economies | 2.3 w | 2 w | 1.8 w | 3058 t | 3670 t | 5154 t | | 35.2 w | 26.3 w | 60.3 w |
| Middle-income economies | 2.3 w | 2.1 w | 1.9 w | 1087 t | 1311 t | 1878 t | | 36 w | 26.8 w | 59.1 w |
| Low-and middle-income econ. | 2.3 w | 2 w | 1.9 w | 4146 t | 4981 t | 7032 t | | 35.4 w | 26.5 w | 60 w |
| Sub-Saharan Africa | 2.7 w | 3.1 w | 3 w | 495 t | 668 t | 1229 t | | 46.4 w | 36.9 w | 50.8 w |
| **East Asia & Pacific** | **2.2 w** | **1.6 w** | **1.4 w** | **1577 t** | **1818 t** | **2276 t** | | **29.5 w** | **21.6 w** | **65.2 w** |
| South Asia | 2.4 w | 2.2 w | 1.8 w | 1148 t | 1377 t | 1896 t | | 38.2 w | 25 w | 57.7 w |
| Europe | 1.1 w | 1 w | 0.8 w | 200 t | 217 t | 252 t | | 26.3 w | 20.4 w | 64.6 w |
| Middle East & N.Africa | 2.8 w | 3.1 w | 2.9 w | 256 t | 341 t | 615 t | | 43.3 w | 34.1 w | 53.4 w |
| Latin America & Caribbean | 2.5 w | 2.1 w | 1.8 w | 433 t | 516 t | 699 t | | 36.2 w | 23.4 w | 59.3 w |
| **EAST ASIA AND PACIFIC** | | | | | | | | | | |
| ***Asian tigers*** | | | | | | | | | | |
| Korea, Rep. | 2 | 1.1 | 0.9 | 43 | 47 | 33 | 56427 | 25.7 | 20.6 | 69.4 |
| Malaysia | 2.5 | 2.6 | 2.3 | 18 | 22 | 32 | 44300 | 38.3 | 23.9 | 58.1 |
| Thailand | 2.9 | 1.8 | 1.4 | 56 | 64 | 84 | 104691 | 33.9 | 21.9 | 63.1 |
| ***Socialist economies in transition*** | | | | | | | | | | |
| Cambodia | 0.3 | 2.6 | 1.9 | 8 | 10 | 14 | 19868 | 34.8 | 26.1 | 62.3 |
| China | 2.2 | 1.4 | 1.3 | 1134 | 1294 | 1597 | 1889676 | 27 | 20.8 | 67.2 |
| Lao P.D.R. | 1.9 | 2.7 | 3.2 | 4 | 6 | 10 | 21436 | 44.8 | 37 | 53.3 |
| Mongolia | 2.6 | 2.8 | 2.5 | 2 | 3 | 4 | 6226 | 40.7 | 25.9 | 55.7 |
| Myanmar | 2.3 | 2.1 | 2 | 42 | 51 | 70 | 96206 | 37.1 | 24 | 58.8 |
| Viet Nam | 2.3 | 2.1 | 2.1 | 66 | 82 | 116 | 159073 | 39.6 | 24.1 | 55.9 |
| ***Large island economies*** | | | | | | | | | | |
| Indonesia | 2.4 | 1.8 | 1.6 | 178 | 209 | 275 | 359557 | 35.8 | 23 | 60.3 |
| Papua New Guinea | 2.4 | 2.5 | 2.3 | 4 | 5 | 7 | 11478 | 41.1 | 27.6 | 56.2 |
| Philippines | 2.8 | 2.4 | 1.8 | 61 | 74 | 101 | 137478 | 39.9 | 23.9 | 56.8 |

| | | | | | | | | | | |
|---|---|---|---|---|---|---|---|---|---|---|
| ***Pacific island economies*** | | | | | | | | | | |
| Fiji | 2.1 | 1.6 | 0.9 | 1 | 1 | 1 | 1279 | 37.2 | 23.1 | 59.7 |
| Kiribati | 1.7 | 1.9 | 1.8 | 0.1 | .. | .. | 176 | 40 | 26.7 | 57.1 |
| Maldives | 3.1 | 3.3 | 3.3 | 0 | 0 | 1 | 1021 | 44.4 | 33.7 | 52.8 |
| Solomon Islands | 3.4 | 3 | 3.2 | 0 | 0 | 1 | 1167 | 45.6 | 28.2 | 51.6 |
| Tonga | 1.4 | 0.5 | 1.2 | 0 | 0 | 0 | 205 | 37.4 | 24 | 58.6 |
| Vanuatu | 3.1 | 2.7 | 3.1 | 0 | 0 | 0 | 577 | 44.4 | 29.3 | 53.6 |
| Western Samoa | 1.2 | 0.6 | 1.6 | 0 | 0 | 0 | 425 | 39.4 | 25.9 | 56.4 |
| ***Other*** | | | | | | | | | | |
| Hong Kong | 2 | 1.4 | 0.8 | 6 | 6 | 7 | 6191 | 21 | 15.4 | 70.2 |
| Japan | 1.2 | 0.6 | 0.3 | 124 | 128 | 128 | 113816 | 18.4 | 15.2 | 69.7 |
| Singapore | 1.6 | 2.2 | 1.2 | 3 | 3 | 4 | 4025 | 23.6 | 18.1 | 70.9 |
| **MEMORANDUM ITEMS** | | | | | | | | | | |
| United States | 1 | 0.9 | 0.8 | 250 | 270 | 307 | 317361 | 21.6 | 18.1 | 66.1 |
| European Community | 0.5 w | 0.3 w | 0.2 w | 344 t | 351 t | 353 t | | 18.2 w | 15.9 w | 67.3 w |
| India | 2.3 | 2.1 | 1.7 | 850 | 1006 | 1348 | 1862082 | 36.9 | 24 | 58.7 |
| Bangladesh | 2.6 | 2.3 | 1.8 | 107 | 128 | 176 | 256545 | 42.9 | 25.7 | 54 |
| Nigeria | 2.5 | 3.2 | 2.8 | 115 | 153 | 255 | 452840 | 46.4 | 32.1 | 51 |
| Tanzania | 2.9 | 3.1 | 3.1 | 25 | 33 | 64 | 145644 | 46.7 | 40.2 | 50.3 |
| Turkey | 2.4 | 2.4 | 1.9 | 56 | 68 | 91 | 119916 | 34.8 | 23.1 | 60.9 |
| Hungary | 0.4 | -0.2 | -0.4 | 11 | 10 | 10 | 10112 | 19.5 | 17.5 | 67 |
| Poland | 0.8 | 0.7 | 0.4 | 38 | 40 | 44 | 50270 | 25.1 | 19.9 | 64.9 |
| Egypt, Arab Rep. | 2.1 | 2.4 | 1.8 | 52 | 62 | 86 | 120472 | 39.2 | 24.4 | 56.6 |
| Argentina | 1.6 | 1.3 | 1 | 32 | 36 | 44 | 53534 | 29.8 | 21.5 | 61.1 |
| Brazil | 2.4 | 2.2 | 1.7 | 150 | 178 | 237 | 305007 | 35.4 | 22.8 | 60.2 |
| Chile | 1.7 | 1.7 | 1.3 | 13 | 15 | 19 | 22738 | 30.5 | 21.3 | 63.6 |
| Mexico | 3.1 | 2 | 1.8 | 86 | 103 | 142 | 184489 | 37.3 | 22.9 | 59 |

a. The projections use the same assumptions as in World Bank 1992e, World Development Indicators.

# Table 23. Demography and Fertility

| Country or group | Crude birth rate per thousand population | | Crude death rate per thousand population | | Women of childbearing age as a percentage of all women | | Total fertility rate | | | Assumed year of reaching net reproduction rate of 1 |
|---|---|---|---|---|---|---|---|---|---|---|
| | *1965* | *1990* | *1965* | *1990* | *1965* | *1990* | *1965* | *1990* | *2000*[a] | |
| **GROUP AVERAGES** | | | | | | | | | | |
| Low-income economies | 42 w | 30 w | 16 w | 10 w | 46 w | 51 w | 6.3 w | 3.8 w | 3.3 w | |
| Middle-income economies | 37 w | 29 w | 12 w | 8 w | 45 w | 49 w | 5.4 w | 3.7 w | 3.2 w | |
| Low-and middle-income econ. | 41 w | 30 w | 15 w | 9 w | 46 w | 50 w | 6.1 w | 3.8 w | 3.2 w | |
| Sub-Saharan Africa | 48 w | 46 w | 23 w | 16 w | 45 w | 44 w | 6.6 w | 6.5 w | 5.9 w | |
| **East Asia & Pacific** | **39 w** | **23 w** | **11 w** | **7 w** | **45 w** | **55 w** | **6.2 w** | **2.7 w** | **2.2 w** | |
| South Asia | 45 w | 32 w | 20 w | 11 w | 47 w | 49 w | 6.3 w | 4.2 w | 3.3 w | |
| Europe | 22 w | 19 w | 10 w | 9 w | 48 w | 49 w | 3.1 w | 2 w | 2.2 w | |
| Middle East & N.Africa | 47 w | 40 w | 20 w | 10 w | 44 w | 46 w | 7.1 w | 5.7 w | 4.8 w | |
| Latin America & Caribbean | 39 w | 27 w | 11 w | 7 w | 45 w | 51 w | 5.8 w | 3.3 w | 2.6 w | |
| **EAST ASIA AND PACIFIC** | | | | | | | | | | |
| ***Asian tigers*** | | | | | | | | | | |
| Korea, Rep. | 35 | 22 | 11 | 5 | 46 | 58 | 4.9 | 2.3 | 2.1 | 1995 |
| Malaysia | 40 | 30 | 12 | 5 | 44 | 50 | 6.3 | 3.8 | 3 | 2015 |
| Thailand | 41 | 22 | 10 | 7 | 44 | 54 | 6.3 | 2.5 | 2.1 | 1995 |
| ***Socialist economies in transition*** | | | | | | | | | | |
| Cambodia | 44 | 38 | 20 | 15 | 47 | 54 | 6.2 | 4.5 | 3.5 | 2015 |
| China | 38 | 22 | 10 | 7 | 45 | 56 | 6.4 | 2.5 | 2.1 | 2000 |
| Lao P.D.R. | 45 | 47 | 23 | 16 | 47 | 45 | 6.1 | 6.7 | 6 | 2040 |
| Mongolia | 43 | 35 | 16 | 8 | 46 | 48 | 5.9 | 4.7 | 3.7 | 2020 |
| Myanmar | 40 | 31 | 18 | 9 | 46 | 50 | 5.8 | 3.8 | 2.9 | 2010 |
| Viet Nam | 39 | 31 | 18 | 7 | 45 | 48 | 6 | 3.8 | 2.9 | 2010 |
| ***Large island economies*** | | | | | | | | | | |
| Indonesia | 43 | 26 | 20 | 9 | 47 | 52 | 5.5 | 3.1 | 2.4 | 2005 |
| Papua New Guinea | 43 | 36 | 20 | 11 | 47 | 48 | 6.2 | 5.1 | 4 | 2020 |
| Philippines | 42 | 29 | 12 | 7 | 44 | 50 | 6.8 | 3.5 | 2.7 | 2010 |

| | | | | | | | | | | |
|---|---|---|---|---|---|---|---|---|---|---|
| ***Pacific island economies*** | | | | | | | | | | |
| Fiji | 35 | 25 | 8 | 7 | 45 | 52 | 5.1 | 3.1 | 2.3 | 2005 |
| Kiribati | 41 | 33 | 8 | 12 | .. | 49 | .. | 4.2 | 3.5 | 2020 |
| Maldives | .. | 43 | .. | 9 | .. | 44 | .. | 6.2 | 5.1 | 2035 |
| Solomon Islands | .. | 38 | .. | 7 | .. | 45 | .. | 5.6 | 4.4 | 2025 |
| Tonga | 41 | 31 | 13 | 6 | .. | 50 | .. | 4 | 3.1 | 2015 |
| Vanuatu | .. | 39 | .. | 8 | .. | 47 | .. | 5.6 | 4.6 | 2030 |
| Western Samoa | .. | 34 | .. | 7 | .. | 47 | .. | 4.6 | 3.6 | 2020 |
| ***Other*** | | | | | | | | | | |
| Hong Kong | 27 | 13 | 6 | 6 | 45 | 56 | 4.5 | 1.5 | 1.5 | 2030 |
| Japan | 19 | 11 | 7 | 7 | 56 | 50 | 2 | 1.6 | 1.6 | 2030 |
| Singapore | 31 | 17 | 6 | 5 | 45 | 60 | 4.7 | 1.9 | 1.9 | 2030 |
| **MEMORANDUM ITEMS** | | | | | | | | | | |
| United States | 19 | 15 | 9 | 9 | 46 | 52 | 2.9 | 1.9 | 1.9 | 2030 |
| European Community | 19 w | 12 w | 11 w | 10 w | 46 w | 49 w | 2.7 w | 1.5 w | 1.6 w | |
| India | 45 | 30 | 20 | 11 | 48 | 49 | 6.2 | 3.9 | 3 | 2015 |
| Bangladesh | 47 | 35 | 21 | 14 | 44 | 47 | 6.8 | 4.6 | 3.3 | 2015 |
| Nigeria | 51 | 43 | 23 | 14 | 45 | 45 | 6.9 | 6 | 5 | 2030 |
| Tanzania | 49 | 48 | 23 | 18 | 45 | 45 | 6.6 | 6.6 | 6.6 | 2045 |
| Turkey | 41 | 28 | 15 | 7 | 45 | 51 | 5.7 | .. | 2.7 | 2010 |
| Hungary | 13 | 12 | 11 | 13 | 48 | 47 | 1.8 | 1.8 | 1.8 | 2030 |
| Poland | 17 | 15 | 7 | 10 | 47 | 48 | 2.5 | 2.1 | 2.1 | 1990 |
| Egypt, Arab Rep. | 43 | 31 | 19 | 10 | 43 | 48 | 6.8 | 4 | 3.1 | 2015 |
| Argentina | 23 | 20 | 9 | 9 | 50 | 47 | 3.1 | 2.8 | 2.3 | 2005 |
| Brazil | 39 | 27 | 11 | 7 | 45 | 52 | 5.6 | 3.2 | 2.4 | 2005 |
| Chile | 34 | 22 | 11 | 6 | 45 | 53 | 4.8 | 2.5 | 2.1 | 2000 |
| Mexico | 45 | 27 | 11 | 5 | 43 | 52 | 6.7 | 3.3 | 2.4 | 2005 |

a. The projections use the same assumptions as in World Bank 1992e, World Development Indicators.

# Table 24. Health and Nutrition

| Country or group | Population per Physician 1965 | Population per Physician 1984 | Population per Nursing person 1965 | Population per Nursing person 1984 | Births attended by health staff (percent) 1985 | Babies with low birth weight (percent) 1985 | Infant mortality rate (per thousand live births) 1965 | Infant mortality rate (per thousand live births) 1990 | Daily calorie supply (per capita) 1965 | Daily calorie supply (per capita) 1989 |
|---|---|---|---|---|---|---|---|---|---|---|
| **GROUP AVERAGES** | | | | | | | | | | |
| Low-income economies | 9640 w | 5800 w | 5980 w | 2150 w | | | 124 w | 69 w | 1975 w | 2406 w |
| Middle-income economies | 3910 w | 2250 w | 2140 w | 970 w | | | 94 w | 48 w | 2489 w | 2860 w |
| Low-and middle-income econ. | 8170 w | 4980 w | 5010 w | 1850 w | | | 117 w | 63 w | 2108 w | 2523 w |
| Sub-Saharan Africa | 33310 w | 26670 w | 5420 w | 2180 w | | | 157 w | 107 w | 2074 w | 2122 w |
| **East Asia & Pacific** | **5600 w** | **2390 w** | **4130 w** | **1530 w** | | | **95 w** | **34 w** | **1939 w** | **2617 w** |
| South Asia | 6220 w | 3460 w | 8380 w | 2650 w | | | 147 w | 93 w | 1992 w | 2215 w |
| Europe | 1260 w | 700 w | 510 w | 480 w | | | 71 w | 30 w | 3069 w | 3433 w |
| Middle East & N.Africa | 7740 w | 2410 w | 6160 w | 1800 w | | | 151 w | 79 w | 2153 w | 3011 w |
| Latin America & Caribbean | 2380 w | 1220 w | 2100 w | 1010 w | | | 94 w | 48 w | 2445 w | 2721 w |
| **EAST ASIA AND PACIFIC** | | | | | | | | | | |
| ***Asian tigers*** | | | | | | | | | | |
| Korea, Rep. | 2680 | 1160 * | 2970 | 580 * | 65 | 9 | 62 | 26 | 2178 | 2852 |
| Malaysia | 6200 | 1930 * | 1320 | 1010 * | 82 | 9 | 55 | 16 | 2353 | 2774 |
| Thailand | 7160 | 6290 * | 4970 | 710 * | 33 | 12 | 88 | 27 | 2138 | 2316 |
| ***Socialist economies in transition*** | | | | | | | | | | |
| Cambodia | 22410 | .. | 3670 | .. | .. | .. | 134 | 117 | 2292 | 2166 |
| China | 1600 | 1010 | 3000 | 1610 | .. | 6 | 90 | 29 | 1929 | 2639 |
| Lao P.D.R. | 24320 | 1360 | 4880 | 530 | .. | 39 | 148 | 103 | 2135 | 2630 |
| Mongolia | 730 | .. | 320 | .. | 99 | 10 | 113 | 62 | 2364 | 2479 |
| Myanmar | 11860 | 3740 | 11370 | 900 | 97 | 16 | 122 | 64 | 1897 | 2440 |
| Viet Nam | .. | 950 * | 14250 * | 590 * | .. | 18 | 134 | 42 | 2041 | 2233 |
| ***Large island economies*** | | | | | | | | | | |
| Indonesia | 31700 | 9410 * | 9490 | .. | 43 | 14 | 128 | 61 | 1791 | 2750 |
| Papua New Guinea | 12640 | 6070 | 620 | 880 | 34 | 25 | 140 | 57 | 1996 | 2403 |
| Philippines | .. | 6570 | 1140 | 2680 * | .. | 18 | 72 | 41 | 1875 | 2375 |

| | | | | | | | | | | |
|---|---|---|---|---|---|---|---|---|---|---|
| ***Pacific island economies*** | | | | | | | | | | |
| Fiji | .. | .. | 890 * | .. | .. | .. | 59 | 24 | 2732 | 2887 |
| Kiribati | .. | 1970 | .. | .. | .. | .. | 121 | 57 | 2170 | 2959 |
| Maldives | .. | .. | .. | .. | .. | .. | .. | 70 | 1710 | 2386 |
| Solomon Islands | .. | 7420 * | .. | .. | .. | .. | .. | 47 | 2253 | 2191 |
| Tonga | .. | .. | .. | 550 | .. | .. | 57 | 22 | 2478 | 2983 |
| Vanuatu | .. | 4990 * | 1000 | 440 * | .. | .. | .. | 69 | 2533 | 2567 |
| Western Samoa | .. | 3600 * | 1060 * | .. | .. | .. | .. | 46 | 2056 | 2509 |
| ***Other*** | | | | | | | | | | |
| Hong Kong | 2520 | 1070 * | 1250 | 240 * | .. | 4 | 27 | 7 | 2486 | 2853 |
| Japan | 970 | 660 * | 410 | 180 * | 100 | 5 | 18 | 5 | 2668 | 2956 |
| Singapore | 1900 | 1410 * | 600 | .. | 100 | 7 | 26 | 7 | 2285 | 3198 |
| **MEMORANDUM ITEMS** | | | | | | | | | | |
| United States | 670 | 470 * | 310 | 70 * | 100 | 7 | 25 | 10 | 3234 | 3671 |
| European Community | 1010 w | 360 w | 600 w | 280 w | | | 27 w | 8 w | 3130 w | 3427 w |
| India | 4880 | 2520 * | 6500 | 1700 * | 33 | 30 | 150 | 92 | 2021 | 2229 |
| Bangladesh | 8100 | 6390 | .. | 8530 | .. | 31 | 144 | 105 | 1970 | 2021 |
| Nigeria | 29530 | 6410 * | 6160 | 900 * | .. | 25 | 162 | 98 | 2185 | 2312 |
| Tanzania | 21700 | 24970 * | 2100 | 5480 * | 74 | 14 | 138 | 115 | 1831 | 2206 |
| Turkey | 2900 | 1390 | .. | 1030 | 78 | 7 | 169 | 60 | 2698 | 3236 |
| Hungary | 630 | 310 | 240 | 170 | 99 | 10 | 39 | 15 | 3134 | 3644 |
| Poland | 800 | 490 | 410 | 190 | .. | 8 | 42 | 16 | 3292 | 3505 |
| Egypt, Arab Rep. | 2300 | 770 * | 2030 | .. | 24 | 7 | 145 | 66 | 2399 | 3336 |
| Argentina | 600 | 370 * | 610 | 980 * | .. | 6 | 58 | 29 | 3163 | 3113 |
| Brazil | 2500 | 1080 * | 3100 * | 1210 * | 73 | 8 | 104 | 57 | 2417 | 2751 |
| Chile | 2120 | 1230 * | 600 | 370 * | 97 | 7 | 98 | 17 | 2581 | 2581 |
| Mexico | 2080 | .. | 980 | 880 * | .. | 15 | 82 | 39 | 2570 | 3052 |

# Table 25. Education

| | Total enrollments as percentage of age group | | | | | | | | | |
|---|---|---|---|---|---|---|---|---|---|---|
| | Primary | | | | Secondary | | | | Tertiary (total) | |
| | Total | | Female | | Total | | Female | | | |
| Country or group | 1965 | 1989 | 1965 | 1989 | 1965 | 1989 | 1965 | 1989 | 1965 | 1989 |
| **GROUP AVERAGES** | | | | | | | | | | |
| Low-income economies | 73 w | 105 w | 47 w | 96 w | 20 w | 38 w | 9 w | 31 w | 1.8 w | 2.7 w |
| Middle-income economies | 93 w | 103 w | 87 w | 101 w | 26 w | 55 w | 23 w | 57 w | 6.5 w | 17 w |
| Low-and middle-income econ. | 78 w | 105 w | 62 w | 97 w | 22 w | 43 w | 14 w | 37 w | 3 w | 7.5 w |
| Sub-Saharan Africa | 41 w | 69 w | 31 w | 61 w | 4 w | 18 w | 2 w | 14 w | 0.2 w | 2.1 w |
| **East Asia & Pacific** | **88 w** | **129 w** | **78 w** | **124 w** | **23 w** | **46 w** | **16 w** | **42 w** | **1.1 w** | **4.8 w** |
| South Asia | 68 w | 90 w | 52 w | 76 w | 24 w | 38 w | 12 w | 27 w | 4.1 w | 4.4 w |
| Europe | 102 w | 102 w | 97 w | 100 w | 45 w | 73 w | 41 w | 70 w | 11.4 w | 16.5 w |
| Middle East & N.Africa | 61 w | 90 w | 43 w | 82 w | 17 w | 53 w | 9 w | 45 w | 3.4 w | 11.6 w |
| Latin America & Caribbean | 98 w | 107 w | 97 w | 107 w | 20 w | 49 w | 19 w | 54 w | 4.4 w | 17.7 w |
| **EAST ASIA AND PACIFIC** | | | | | | | | | | |
| ***Asian tigers*** | | | | | | | | | | |
| Korea, Rep. | 101 | 108 | 99 | 109 | 35 | 86 | 25 | 84 | 6 | 38 |
| Malaysia | 90 | 96 | 84 | 96 | 28 | 59 | 22 | 59 | 2 | 6.6 * |
| Thailand | 78 | 86 | 74 | .. | 14 | 28 * | 11 | .. | 2 | 16.1 |
| ***Socialist economies in transition*** | | | | | | | | | | |
| Cambodia | 77 | .. | 56 | .. | 9 | .. | 4 | .. | 1 | .. |
| China | 89 | 135 | .. | 128 | 24 * | 44 | .. | 38 | 0.1 | 1.7 |
| Lao P.D.R. | 40 | 111 * | 30 | 98 * | 2 | 27 * | 1 | 22 * | 0.1 | 1.6 * |
| Mongolia | 98 | 98 | 97 | 100 | 66 | .. | 66 | .. | 8 | .. |
| Myanmar | 71 | 103 * | 65 | 100 * | 15 | 24 * | 11 | 23 * | 1 | 4.8 * |
| Viet Nam | .. | .. | .. | .. | .. | .. | .. | .. | .. | .. |
| ***Large island economies*** | | | | | | | | | | |
| Indonesia | 72 | 118 * | 65 | 115 * | 12 | 47 * | 7 | 43 * | 1 | .. |
| Papua New Guinea | 44 | 73 | 35 | 67 | 4 | 13 | 2 | 10 | .. | .. |
| Philippines | 113 | 111 | 111 | 110 | 41 | 73 | 40 | 75 | 19 | 28.2 * |

| | | | | | | | | | | |
|---|---|---|---|---|---|---|---|---|---|---|
| ***Pacific island economies*** | | | | | | | | | | |
| Fiji | 85 | .. | 82 | .. | 20 | .. | 15 | .. | .. | .. |
| Kiribati | .. | .. | .. | .. | .. | .. | .. | .. | .. | .. |
| Maldives | .. | .. | .. | .. | .. | .. | .. | .. | .. | .. |
| Solomon Islands | .. | .. | .. | .. | .. | .. | .. | .. | .. | .. |
| Tonga | .. | .. | .. | .. | .. | .. | .. | .. | .. | .. |
| Vanuatu | .. | .. | .. | .. | .. | .. | .. | .. | .. | .. |
| Western Samoa | .. | .. | .. | .. | .. | .. | .. | .. | .. | .. |
| ***Other*** | | | | | | | | | | |
| Hong Kong | 103 | 105 * | 99 | 104 * | 29 | 73 * | 25 | 75 * | 5 | .. |
| Japan | 100 | 102 | 100 | 102 | 82 | 96 | 81 | 97 | 13 | 30.7 |
| Singapore | 105 | 110 | 100 | 109 | 45 | 69 | 41 | 71 | 10 | .. |
| **MEMORANDUM ITEMS** | | | | | | | | | | |
| United States | 100 | .. | .. | .. | .. | .. | .. | .. | 40 | 63.1 * |
| European Community | 110 w | 106 w | 109 w | 105 w | 55 w | 91 w | 51 w | 93 w | 12.3 w | 30.3 w |
| India | 74 | 98 | 57 | 82 | 27 | 43 | 13 | 31 | 5 | .. |
| Bangladesh | 49 | 70 | 31 | 64 | 13 | 17 | 3 | 11 | 1 | 3.6 |
| Nigeria | 32 | 70 | 24 | 63 | 5 | 19 | 3 | 16 | 0.1 | 3.2 * |
| Tanzania | 32 | 63 | 25 | 63 | 2 | 4 | 1 | 4 | 0.1 | 0.2 |
| Turkey | 101 | 112 | 83 | 108 | 16 | 51 | 9 | 39 | 4 | 12.7 |
| Hungary | 101 | 94 | 100 | 94 | .. | 76 | .. | 77 | 13 | 14.7 |
| Poland | 104 | 99 | 102 | 99 | 69 | 81 | 69 | 83 | 18 | 20.3 |
| Egypt, Arab Rep. | 75 | 97 | 60 | 89 | 26 | 81 | 15 | 71 | 7 | 19.6 * |
| Argentina | 101 | 111 * | 102 | 114 * | 28 | 74 * | 31 | 78 * | 14 | 40.8 * |
| Brazil | 108 | 105 | 108 | .. | 16 | 39 | 16 | 45 * | 2 | 11.2 |
| Chile | 124 | 100 | 122 | 99 | 34 | 75 | 36 | 78 | 6 | 18.8 * |
| Mexico | 92 | 114 | 90 | 112 | 17 | 53 | 13 | 53 | 4 | 14.6 |

# Table 26. Urbanization

| Country or group | Urban population: As a percentage of total population | | Urban population: Average annual growth rate (percent) | | Population in capital city as a percentage of: Urban | Population in capital city as a percentage of: Total | Population in cities of 1 million or more in 1990, as a percentage of: Urban | | Total | |
|---|---|---|---|---|---|---|---|---|---|---|
| | 1965 | 1990 | 1965–80 | 1980–90 | 1990 | 1990 | 1965 | 1990 | 1965 | 1990 |
| **GROUP AVERAGES** | | | | | | | | | | |
| Low-income economies | 18 w | 38 w | 3.5 w | 9 w | 11 w | 3 w | 41 w | 31 w | 7 w | 9 w |
| Middle-income economies | 42 w | 60 w | 3.9 w | 3.4 w | 25 w | 14 w | 41 w | 40 w | 17 w | 25 w |
| Low-and middle-income econ. | 24 w | 44 w | 3.7 w | 6.6 w | 15 w | 6 w | 41 w | 33 w | 10 w | 13 w |
| Sub-Saharan Africa | 14 w | 29 w | 5.8 w | 5.9 w | 32 w | 9 w | 30 w | 29 w | 4 w | 9 w |
| **East Asia & Pacific** | **19 w** | **50 w** | **3 w** | **12 w** | **9 w** | **3 w** | **48 w** | **30 w** | **9 w** | **11 w** |
| South Asia | 18 w | 26 w | 3.9 w | 3.9 w | 8 w | 2 w | 35 w | 34 w | 6 w | 9 w |
| Europe | 40 w | 60 w | 2.7 w | 2.6 w | 15 w | 10 w | 31 w | 27 w | 12 w | 16 w |
| Middle East & N.Africa | 35 w | 51 w | 4.6 w | 4.4 w | 27 w | 13 w | 42 w | 42 w | 15 w | 21 w |
| Latin America & Caribbean | 53 w | 71 w | 3.9 w | 3 w | 23 w | 16 w | 44 w | 45 w | 24 w | 33 w |
| **EAST ASIA AND PACIFIC** | | | | | | | | | | |
| ***Asian tigers*** | | | | | | | | | | |
| Korea, Rep. | 32 | 72 | 5.8 | 3.5 | 36 | 26 | 74 | 69 | 24 | 50 |
| Malaysia | 26 | 43 | 4.6 | 4.9 | 22 | 10 | 16 | 22 | 4 | 10 |
| Thailand | 13 | 23 | 5.1 | 4.6 | 57 | 13 | 66 | 57 | 8 | 13 |
| ***Socialist economies in transition*** | | | | | | | | | | |
| Cambodia | 11 | 12 | -0.4 | 3.8 | 98 | 11 | .. | .. | .. | .. |
| China | 18 | 56 | 2.3 | 14.9 | 2 | 1 | 49 | 27 | 9 | 9 |
| Lao P.D.R. | 8 | 19 | 5.3 | 6.1 | 53 | 10 | .. | .. | .. | .. |
| Mongolia | 42 | 52 | 4 | 2.9 | 42 | 22 | .. | .. | .. | .. |
| Myanmar | 21 | 25 | 3.2 | 2.4 | 32 | 8 | 23 | 32 | 5 | 8 |
| Viet Nam | 16 | 22 | 3.3 | 3.4 | 22 | 5 | 37 | 30 | 6 | 7 |
| ***Large island economies*** | | | | | | | | | | |
| Indonesia | 16 | 31 | 4.8 | 5.1 | 17 | 5 | 42 | 33 | 7 | 10 |
| Papua New Guinea | 5 | 16 | 8.2 | 4.5 | 32 | 5 | .. | .. | .. | .. |
| Philippines | 32 | 43 | 4 | 3.8 | 32 | 14 | 28 | 32 | 9 | 14 |

| | | | | | | | | | | |
|---|---|---|---|---|---|---|---|---|---|---|
| ***Pacific island economies*** | | | | | | | | | | |
| Fiji | 33 | 44 | 3.3 | 3 | 61 | 27 | .. | .. | .. | .. |
| Kiribati | 20 | 36 | 4.7 | 3.3 | 95 | 34 | .. | .. | .. | .. |
| Maldives | 12 | 29 | 8 | 6.2 | 100 | 29 | .. | .. | .. | .. |
| Solomon Islands | 9 | 11 | 3.7 | 4.5 | 90 | 9 | .. | .. | .. | .. |
| Tonga | 21 | 21 | 0.9 | 0.9 | 123 | 25 | .. | .. | .. | .. |
| Vanuatu | 11 | 20 | 6.8 | 4 | 82 | 17 | .. | .. | .. | .. |
| Western Samoa | 19 | 23 | 1.9 | 1.3 | 98 | 22 | .. | .. | .. | .. |
| ***Other*** | | | | | | | | | | |
| Hong Kong | 89 | 94 | 2.1 | 1.7 | 100 | 94 | 90 | 99 | 81 | 93 |
| Japan | 67 | 77 | 2.1 | 0.7 | 19 | 15 | 37 | 36 | 25 | 27 |
| Singapore | 100 | 100 | 1.6 | 2.2 | 91 | 91 | 73 | 100 | 73 | 100 |
| **MEMORANDUM ITEMS** | | | | | | | | | | |
| United States | 72 | 75 | 1.2 | 1.1 | 2 | 1 | 49 | 48 | 35 | 36 |
| European Community | 71 w | 78 w | 0.9 w | 0.5 w | 17 w | 10 w | 30 w | 26 w | 21 w | 20 w |
| India | 19 | 27 | 3.7 | 3.7 | 4 | 1 | 32 | 32 | 6 | 9 |
| Bangladesh | 6 | 16 | 6.8 | 6.2 | 38 | 6 | 50 | 47 | 3 | 8 |
| Nigeria | 17 | 35 | 5.7 | 6 | 19 | 7 | 23 | 24 | 4 | 8 |
| Tanzania | 5 | 33 | 11.3 | 10.5 | 21 | 7 | 38 | 18 | 2 | 6 |
| Turkey | 34 | 61 | 4.1 | 5.9 | 8 | 5 | 41 | 35 | 14 | 22 |
| Hungary | 43 | 61 | 1.9 | 1.2 | 33 | 20 | 43 | 33 | 19 | 20 |
| Poland | 50 | 62 | 1.9 | 1.3 | 9 | 6 | 32 | 28 | 16 | 18 |
| Egypt, Arab Rep. | 41 | 47 | 2.7 | 3.1 | 37 | 17 | 53 | 52 | 22 | 24 |
| Argentina | 76 | 86 | 2.2 | 1.8 | 41 | 36 | 53 | 49 | 40 | 42 |
| Brazil | 50 | 75 | 4.3 | 3.4 | 2 | 2 | 48 | 47 | 24 | 35 |
| Chile | 72 | 86 | 2.6 | 2.3 | 42 | 36 | 39 | 42 | 28 | 36 |
| Mexico | 55 | 73 | 4.4 | 2.9 | 32 | 23 | 41 | 45 | 22 | 32 |

# Table 27. Women in Development

| Country or group | Health and welfare: Under-5 mortality rate (per 1,000 live births) Female 1990 | Male 1990 | Life expectancy at birth (years) Female 1965 | Female 1990 | Male 1965 | Male 1990 | Maternal mortality (per 100,000 live births) 1980 | Education (percentage of cohort persisting to grade 4) Female 1970 | Female 1985 | Male 1970 |
|---|---|---|---|---|---|---|---|---|---|---|
| **GROUP AVERAGES** | | | | | | | | | | |
| Low-income economies | 91 w | 97 w | 50 w | 62 w | 48 w | 61 w | 389 w | 53 w | 73 w | 58 w |
| Middle-income economies | 56 w | 67 w | 60 w | 69 w | 56 w | 64 w | 158 w | 78 w | 87 w | 77 w |
| Low-and middle-income econ. | 82 w | 89 w | 52 w | 64 w | 50 w | 62 w | 333 w | 61 w | 77 w | 65 w |
| Sub-Saharan Africa | 160 w | 179 w | 43 w | 52 w | 41 w | 49 w | 952 w | 66 w | 70 w | 69 w |
| **East Asia & Pacific** | **37 w** | **48 w** | **55 w** | **70 w** | **52 w** | **67 w** | **142 w** | **73 w** | **78 w** | **86 w** |
| South Asia | 126 w | 119 w | 45 w | 58 w | 46 w | 59 w | 498 w | 45 w | 47 w | 48 w |
| Europe | 34 w | 40 w | 68 w | 74 w | 63 w | 67 w | 84 w | 90 w | 98 w | 93 w |
| Middle East & N.Africa | 102 w | 117 w | 49 w | 62 w | 48 w | 60 w | 408 w | 81 w | 89 w | 85 w |
| Latin America & Caribbean | 52 w | 64 w | 60 w | 71 w | 56 w | 65 w | 138 w | 64 w | 74 w | 59 w |
| **EAST ASIA AND PACIFIC** | | | | | | | | | | |
| ***Asian tigers*** | | | | | | | | | | |
| Korea, Rep. | 17 | 24 | 58 | 73 | 55 | 67 | 34 | 96 | 99 | 96 |
| Malaysia | 17 | 22 | 60 | 72 | 56 | 68 | 59 | .. | .. | .. |
| Thailand | 28 | 38 | 58 | 68 | 54 | 63 | 270 | 71 | .. | 69 |
| ***Socialist economies in transition*** | | | | | | | | | | |
| Cambodia | 161 | 180 | 46 | 52 | 43 | 49 | .. | .. | .. | .. |
| China | 29 | 40 | 57 | 71 | 53 | 69 | 44 | .. | 76 | .. |
| Lao P.D.R. | 159 | 179 | 42 | 51 | 39 | 48 | .. | .. | .. | .. |
| Mongolia | 76 | 91 | 51 | 64 | 49 | 61 | 140 | .. | .. | .. |
| Myanmar | 78 | 94 | 49 | 64 | 46 | 59 | 140 | 39 | .. | 58 |
| Viet Nam | 46 | 59 | 51 | 69 | 48 | 64 | 110 | .. | .. | .. |
| ***Large island economies*** | | | | | | | | | | |
| Indonesia | 75 | 90 | 45 | 64 | 43 | 60 | 800 | 67 * | 83 | 89 * |
| Papua New Guinea | 70 | 84 | 44 | 56 | 44 | 54 | 1000 | 76 | .. | 84 |
| Philippines | 45 | 57 | 57 | 66 | 54 | 62 | 80 | .. | 82 | .. |

| | | | | | | | | | | |
|---|---|---|---|---|---|---|---|---|---|---|
| ***Pacific island economies*** | | | | | | | | | | |
| Fiji | 24 | 33 | 57 | 67 | 54 | 63 | 47 | 97 | 95 * | 94 |
| Kiribati | 80 | 93 | .. | 57 | .. | 53 | .. | .. | 88 | .. |
| Maldives | 88 | 105 | .. | 63 | .. | 60 | .. | .. | .. | .. |
| Solomon Islands | 63 | 75 | .. | 65 | .. | 64 | .. | .. | .. | .. |
| Tonga | 22 | 31 | .. | 69 | .. | 65 | .. | .. | 98 * | .. |
| Vanuatu | 87 | 95 | .. | 66 | .. | 63 | .. | 72 | .. | 75 |
| Western Samoa | 53 | 66 | .. | 69 | .. | 64 | .. | .. | .. | .. |
| ***Other*** | | | | | | | | | | |
| Hong Kong | 7 | 10 | 71 | 80 | 64 | 75 | 4 | 94 | .. | 92 |
| Japan | 5 | 7 | 73 | 82 | 68 | 76 | 15 | 100 | 100 | 100 |
| Singapore | 7 | 10 | 68 | 77 | 64 | 71 | 11 | 99 | 100 | 99 |
| **MEMORANDUM ITEMS** | | | | | | | | | | |
| United States | 10 | 13 | 74 | 80 | 67 | 73 | 9 | .. | 96 * | .. |
| European Community | 9 w | 12 w | 74 w | 80 w | 68 w | 73 w | 11 w | 93 w | 97 w | 91 w |
| India | 121 | 116 | 44 | 58 | 46 | 60 | 500 | 42 | .. | 45 |
| Bangladesh | 160 | 142 | 44 | 51 | 45 | 52 | 600 | .. | 40 | .. |
| Nigeria | 152 | 171 | 43 | 54 | 40 | 49 | 1500 | 64 | .. | 66 |
| Tanzania | 182 | 203 | 45 | 49 | 41 | 46 | 370 | 82 | 91 | 88 |
| Turkey | 73 | 80 | 55 | 69 | 52 | 64 | 207 | 76 | 98 | 81 |
| Hungary | 16 | 22 | 72 | 75 | 67 | 67 | 28 | 90 | 97 | 99 |
| Poland | 18 | 23 | 72 | 75 | 66 | 67 | 12 | 99 | .. | 97 |
| Egypt, Arab Rep. | 95 | 110 | 50 | 62 | 48 | 59 | 500 | 85 | .. | 93 |
| Argentina | 30 | 40 | 69 | 75 | 63 | 68 | 85 | 92 | .. | 69 |
| Brazil | 62 | 75 | 59 | 69 | 55 | 63 | 150 | 56 * | .. | 54 * |
| Chile | 18 | 23 | 63 | 76 | 57 | 69 | 55 | 86 | 96 * | 83 |
| Mexico | 41 | 51 | 61 | 73 | 58 | 66 | 92 | .. | 73 | .. |

## Table 28. Regional Performance Indicators, 1965–90

| *Region and indicator* | *Average annual growth rate (percent)* "Intervention" era 1965–80 | "Reform" era 1980–90 |
|---|---|---|
| **EAST ASIA** | | |
| GDP | 7.3 | 7.8 |
| Industry | 10.8 | 10.2 |
| Gross domestic investment | 11.1 | 10.6 |
| Exports | 8.5 | 9.8 |
| Inflation | 9.3 | 6.0 |
| **SOUTH ASIA** | | |
| GDP | 3.6 | 5.2 |
| Industry | 4.3 | 6.5 |
| Gross domestic investment | 4.1 | 4.6 |
| Exports | 1.8 | 6.8 |
| Inflation | 8.3 | 8.0 |
| **SUB-SAHARAN AFRICA** | | |
| GDP | 4.2 | 2.1 |
| Industry | 7.2 | 2.0 |
| Gross domestic investment | 8.7 | -4.3 |
| Exports | 6.1 | 0.2 |
| Inflation | 11.4 | 20.0 |
| **LATIN AMERICA AND CARIBBEAN** | | |
| GDP | 6.0 | 1.6 |
| Industry | 6.6 | 1.2 |
| Gross domestic investment | 8.2 | -2.0 |
| Exports | -1.0 | 3.0 |
| Inflation | 31.4 | 192.1 |
| **LOW- AND MIDDLE-INCOME COUNTRIES** | | |
| GDP | 5.9 | 3.2 |
| Industry | 6.8 | 3.8 |
| Gross domestic investment | 8.3 | 2.3 |
| Exports | 4.1 | 4.1 |
| Inflation | 16.7 | 61.8 |

*Source*: World Bank 1992e.

# Table 29. Classification of Economies by Income and Region, 1992–93

| | | *Sub-Saharan Africa* | | *Asia* | | *Europe and Central Asia* | | *Middle East and North Africa* | | |
|---|---|---|---|---|---|---|---|---|---|---|
| *Income group* | *Subgroup* | *East & Southern Africa* | *West Africa* | *East Asia and Pacific* | *South Asia* | *Eastern Europe and Central Asia* | *Rest of Europe* | *Middle East* | *North Africa* | *Americas* |
| *Low-income* | | Burundi<br>Comoros<br>Ethiopia<br>Kenya<br>Lesotho<br>Madagascar<br>Malawi<br>Mozambique<br>Rwanda<br>Somalia<br>Sudan<br>Tanzania<br>Uganda<br>Zaire<br>Zambia<br>Zimbabwe | Benin<br>Burkina Faso<br>Central African Rep.<br>Chad<br>Equatorial Guinea<br>Gambia, The<br>Ghana<br>Guinea<br>Guinea-Bissau<br>Liberia<br>Mali<br>Mauritania<br>Niger<br>Nigeria<br>São Tomé and Principe<br>Sierra Leone<br>Togo | Cambodia<br>China<br>Indonesia<br>Lao PDR<br>Myanmar<br>Solomon Islands<br>Viet Nam | Afghanistan<br>Bangladesh<br>Bhutan<br>India<br>Maldives<br>Nepal<br>Pakistan<br>Sri Lanka | | | Yemen, Rep. | Egypt, Arab Rep. | Guyana<br>Haiti<br>Honduras<br>Nicaragua |
| *Middle-income* | *Lower* | Angola<br>Djibouti<br>Mauritius<br>Namibia<br>Swaziland | Cameroon<br>Cape Verde<br>Congo<br>Côte d'Ivoire<br>Senegal | Fiji<br>Kiribati<br>Korea, Dem. Rep.<br>Malaysia<br>Marshall Islands<br>Micronesia, Fed. Sts.<br>Mongolia<br>Papua New Guinea<br>Philippines<br>Thailand<br>Tonga<br>Vanuatu<br>Western Samoa | | Albania<br>Armenia<br>Azerbaijan<br>Bulgaria<br>Czecho-slovakia[a]<br>Georgia<br>Kazakhstan<br>Kyrgyzstan<br>Moldova<br>Poland<br>Romania<br>Tajikistan<br>Turkmenistan<br>Ukraine<br>Uzbekistan | Turkey | Iran, Islamic Rep.<br>Iraq<br>Jordan<br>Lebanon<br>Syrian Arab Rep. | Algeria<br>Morocco<br>Tunisia | Belize<br>Bolivia<br>Chile<br>Colombia<br>Costa Rica<br>Cuba<br>Dominica<br>Dominican Rep.<br>Ecuador<br>El Salvador<br>Grenada<br>Guatemala<br>Jamaica<br>Panama<br>Paraguay<br>Peru<br>St. Lucia<br>St. Vincent |
| | *Upper* | Botswana<br>Mayotte<br>Reunion<br>Seychelles<br>South Africa | Gabon | American Samoa<br>Guam<br>Korea, Rep.<br>Macao<br>New Caledonia | | Belarus<br>Estonia<br>Hungary<br>Latvia<br>Lithuania<br>Russian Federation<br>Yugoslavia[b] | Gibraltar<br>Greece<br>Isle of Man<br>Malta<br>Portugal | Bahrain<br>Oman<br>Saudi Arabia | Libya | Antigua and Barbuda<br>Argentina<br>Aruba<br>Barbados<br>Brazil<br>French Guiana<br>Guadeloupe<br>Martinique<br>Mexico<br>Netherlands Antilles<br>Puerto Rico<br>St. Kitts and Nevis<br>Suriname<br>Trinidad and Tobago<br>Uruguay<br>Venezuela |
| *No. of low- & middle-income economies:* 162 | | 26 | 23 | 25 | 8 | 22 | 6 | 9 | 5 | 38 |

*(Table continues on the following page)*

## Table 29 *(continued)*

| Income group | Subgroup | Sub-Saharan Africa: East & Southern Africa | Sub-Saharan Africa: West Africa | Asia: East Asia and Pacific | Asia: South Asia | Europe and Central Asia: Eastern Europe and Central Asia | Europe and Central Asia: Rest of Europe | Middle East and North Africa: Middle East | Middle East and North Africa: North Africa | Americas |
|---|---|---|---|---|---|---|---|---|---|---|
| High-income | OECD countries | | | Australia<br>Japan<br>New Zealand | | | Andorra<br>Austria<br>Belgium<br>Denmark<br>Finland<br>France<br>Germany<br>Iceland<br>Ireland<br>Italy<br>Luxembourg<br>Netherlands<br>Norway<br>San Marino<br>Spain<br>Sweden<br>Switzerland<br>United Kingdom | | | Canada<br>United States |
| | Non-OECD countries | | | Brunei<br>French Polynesia<br>Hong Kong<br>Singapore<br>OAE[c] | | | Channel Islands<br>Cyprus<br>Faeroe Islands<br>Greenland | Israel<br>Kuwait<br>Qatar<br>United Arab Emirates | | Bahamas<br>Bermuda<br>Virgin Islands (US) |
| Total no. of economies: | 201 | 26 | 23 | 33 | 8 | 22 | 28 | 13 | 5 | 43 |

a. Refers to the former Czechoslovakia, because disaggregated data are not yet available.
b. Refers to the former Socialist Federal Republic of Yugoslavia, because disaggregated data are not yet available.
c. Other Asian economies—Taiwan, China.

### Definitions of groups

These tables classify all World Bank member economies, plus all other economies with populations of more than 30,000.

*Income group:* Economies are divided according to 1991 GNP per capita, calculated using the *World Bank Atlas* method. The groups are: low-income, $635 or less; lower-middle-income, $636–2,555; upper-middle-income, $2,556–$7,909; and high-income, $7,910 or more.

The estimates for the republics of the former Soviet Union should be regarded as very preliminary; their classification will be kept under review.

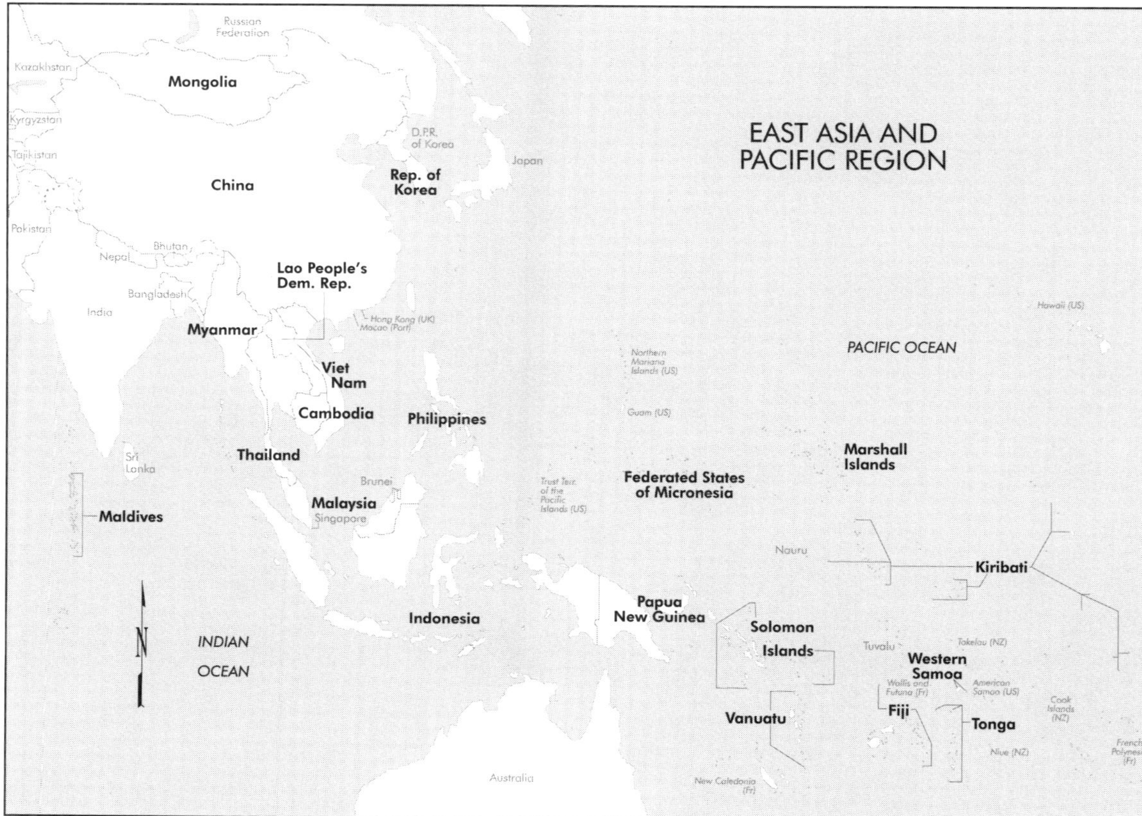
EAST ASIA AND
PACIFIC REGION
Russian Federation
Kazakhstan
Kyrgyzstan
Tajikistan
Pakistan
Mongolia
China
D.P.R. of Korea
Rep. of Korea
Japan
Nepal
Bhutan
Bangladesh
India
Lao People's Dem. Rep.
Myanmar
Hong Kong (UK)
Macao (Port)
Viet Nam
Cambodia
Philippines
Thailand
Sri Lanka
Brunei
Malaysia
Singapore
Maldives
Indonesia
INDIAN
OCEAN
N
PACIFIC OCEAN
Hawaii (US)
Northern Mariana Islands (US)
Guam (US)
Trust Terr. of the Pacific Islands (US)
Federated States of Micronesia
Marshall Islands
Nauru
Kiribati
Papua New Guinea
Solomon Islands
Tuvalu
Tokelau (NZ)
Western Samoa
Wallis and Futuna (Fr)
American Samoa (US)
Fiji
Tonga
Cook Islands (NZ)
Vanuatu
Niue (NZ)
French Polynesia (Fr)
New Caledonia (Fr)
Australia